FIRE IN MY BELLY

FIRE

in My Belly

Alfred J. Roach

WOLFHOUND PRESS

Published in 1998 by
Wolfhound Press Ltd
68 Mountjoy Square
Dublin 1, Ireland
Tel: (353-1) 874 0354
Fax: (353-1) 872 0207

British Library Cataloguing in Publication Data
A catalogue record for this book is available from the British Library.

ISBN 0-86327-678-4

10 9 8 7 6 5 4 3 2 1

Picture Acknowledgements
The publishers have made every reasonable effort to contact the copyright holders of
photographs reproduced in this book. If any involuntary infringement of copyright has
occurred, sincere apologies are offered and the owners of such copyright are requested
to contact the publishers. For permission to reproduce pictures we gratefully acknowl-
edge the following:
Cover photographs: Phil Carrick
Fireman graphic: Shane Fletcher
p. 49: Bachrach, New York

Picture Section
p. 2 (top): *Buffalo Courier*
p. 4 (bottom): Shane Fletcher
p. 9: Joyce Ravid in *Forbes* magazine
p. 11 (top): Bill Fitzpatrick, White House
p. 8 (both pictures), p. 13 (both pictures), p. 15 (top), p. 16 (both pictures): Phil Carrick
p. 15 (bottom): Bill Doyle

Cover Photographs: Phil Carrick
Cover Design: Slick Fish Design
Typesetting: Wolfhound Press
Printed in the Republic of Ireland by Colour Books, Dublin.

Contents

Dedication

*To my mother Nellie,
my eternal gratitude to the woman who lit my fire,
and to my wife Dorothy
who stoked that fire for more than fifty years.*

Acknowledgements

For more than ten years, people have been urging me to put my life story on paper. I've always resisted. Hell, I've got plenty more life to live! And, I still believe that to be true. But, when you reach the age of 82, and your house-keeper won't buy you green bananas any more, and the hash-slinger at the local diner won't sell you a three-minute egg without getting paid up front ... then, it's time to fill your fountain pen and start jotting down your memoirs.

Of all the people who have encouraged me to author a book, none has been more insistent nor more persuasive than a daughter of Ireland, Ellena Byrne, originally of Myshall, Co. Carlow, and now of Dublin and of ABS. It was Ellena who was the strongest voice urging me to write a book. For the present work, Ellena has performed an especially demanding role. From beginning to end, she demonstrated her administrative skill in orchestrating every detail with the publisher, with outside profession-als, and with the people who have been such supportive and effective colleagues to me over the years. Experts who know the book industry from A to Z say Ellena is the best inside co-ordinator for a book project they have seen, and I believe that easily since Ellena strives for the excep-tional in all she tackles. But all of us have our limits, and that's how I was able to sneak in a little surprise in Chap-ter 9, which even Ellena's watchful eye didn't catch.

My family has been an important source of inspiration and support for me over the years. My wife Dorothy shared her memories and our goals in raising a family and building a business. My son AP added several worthwhile geopolitical insights to the manuscript and showed his Information Age skills by verifying a number of facts for me through accessing the Internet. My son Tim, TII's president, has an exceptional knack for details and was especially helpful in reconstructing important events in TII's history. My daughter Dorothy contributed her customary perceptiveness in recalling the years in which the family grew up. We have been blessed with nine grandchildren and three great-grandchildren. It wasn't possible to involve all of them in the writing of this book, but Tim's daughter Stacey was an able spokesperson for the coming generations. I must confess that there have been two loves in my life — the lady I married 55 years ago, Dorothy my wife; and the other love affair that goes back over 75 years to when, as a young boy of 8, I was introduced to the Dominican Sisters. Both loves continue to exert positive forces in my life. Among all the family members, my deepest thanks in the research for this book go to my sister Margaret, whom the world knows as Sister Ellen Cecile. She was a wonderful source of information and insight about our early years in Harlem and Brooklyn.

People I have known for years — and who have helped make me whatever success I may be today — recalled our work together for the benefit of the book. They include Dorothy Conboy, Frank Schleip, Al Dockweiler, and Charlie Roberts. Others who contributed were current members of the TII team, including Bruce Barksdale, John Hyland (and, of course, I must mention his wife Brenda), Carl Meyerhoefer, Nisar Chaudhry, Jim Roach, Gini Hall, and Laura Gavey in New York, and Greg Cortes, José Ramon Garcia, Bartolo Alcantara, Irma Lopez, and Isabel Perez in the Caribbean.

ABS, the other company of which I am currently chairman, has a remarkable array of scientific talent on its Advisory Board, and I am humbled that distinguished scientists of global stature — such as Professor Gustav Born in London, Professor Heinz Nau in Hanover, and Professor Rem Petrov in Moscow — took time out from their demanding schedules to help me with this project. Professor Peter Morozov in Moscow and Marina Dorokhova in St Petersburg also contributed valued co-ordinating support. Members of ABS's management — including Dr Stephen Ip, Dr Emer Leahy, and Dr Jim McLinden — helped keep me abreast of the latest scientific developments in areas where I am a novice, even though a passionate one. The woman of the hour at ABS in New York was my administrative assistant, Teri Kroll, who co-ordinated the flow of meetings and support logistics with a sure hand and seemingly without effort.

The manuscript benefited from the comments of some astute readers, all of whom are good friends, but who — true to real friendship — also had the wisdom and judgment to tell me when I was headed astray: Dr Bill Sharwell, former Congressman Jim Grover, Dr Emer Leahy, Professor Peter Morozov, and especially Professor Ciaran Regan, whose comments were particularly detailed and penetrating. Mr James Kirwan also gave the manuscript a greatly appreciated reading.

No project of this scale ever gets done without the help of devoted specialists who are not involved in the actual writing of the book. Without a doubt, Barbara Moss occupies the place of honour among specialists — housekeeper *extraordinaire* and photo archivist *exceptionnelle*. Dr Pablo Morales kindly reviewed the section on prostate cancer in Chapter 8 and Dr Stephen L. DeFelice read the Appendix section entitled 'Volcanoes'. Tom Gleason added engaging recollections of his father, Teddy — a man who helped steer my thinking in new directions. Tom Geraghty contributed some useful insights on the history of firefighting, and Jeff Kocar did so on the history of railroading. Several lawyers gave esteemed counsel during various stages of the book development, including Jim Grover, Tom Hyland, Patricia McGovern, and Jessica Friedman. Stephen Doak showed what a broad palette he has in his grasp, ranging from computer graphics to just the right stanza of poetry.

Last, but surely not least, are my colleagues at Wolfhound Press. My thanks to Seamus Cashman for his confidence in the concept and his willingness to explore a fresh path in the Irish marketplace, to Emer Ryan for her astute eye and her useful guidance on keeping the text clear and consistent, and to the Wolfhound sales and marketing team for the efforts they are preparing to make on behalf of this book.

What you are about to read is *not* the story of an exceptional person. It is the record of the exceptional things that can happen when an ordinary guy with determination gives his imagination free rein.

Prologue

'Take the hill. Take the goddamn hill,' I shouted at the ex-Marine who we recently tapped to be Executive Vice-President and Chief Operating Officer at TII, a telecommunications manufacturing company I started thirty-five years ago. 'And, George,' I paused for emphasis, 'send me the report about how you intend to do it *after* you have done it.' George, with his team from Puerto Rico, was on an aeroplane that Friday night to fix the problem. Indeed, he 'took the hill'.

Touring our factory in the Dominican Republic the day before, I had seen things that didn't appeal to my eighty-two-year-old eyes. In this plant, we assemble lightning surge protectors to safeguard phone lines (and the people who use them) from lightning strikes and other dangerous electrical surges. The eight hundred people were energised, and the plant was humming to the steady beat of *merengue* music pulsing over the loudspeaker system. Quality control — so vital to this precision business — was in tip-top shape, but the receiving and shipping area wasn't as tidy as it should have been, and other operating disciplines needed a tune-up.

I knew the fault didn't lie with Bartolo Alcantara, our VP of Operations in the Dominican Republic. An amazing fellow, Bartolo took four years to advance from the fifth to the sixth grade as his family eked out a living in an impoverished village. For half his life, Bartolo never had any contact with any telecommunications equipment. He was nineteen before he dialled his first telephone. Today he has three university degrees (including an MBA), teaches

English at night, and helps his wife run a remarkable multinational school for youngsters, which couples state of the art electronics with open-windowed classrooms ventilated by swaying palm trees.

Bartolo was and is *Mr Energy* — but I knew that he couldn't do it alone. Nor did the trouble lie with my son Tim, President of TII, who has long headed TII's day-to-day operations out of New York with a masterful knack for administration and planning as well as marketing and finance. Still, it was clear that we needed another hand in the business to help out. So, we lured a seasoned executive to us — George Katsarakes — whom I liked for his blend of worldly wisdom and fire in his belly. Even though in his early sixties, George is a mere kid in comparison with me. With our resources beefed up, the business was back on track, and I receded into the background, as I normally do when things are humming as they should be.

Our success as a manufacturer in the Caribbean has been very much an issue of the high-quality people who have been members of our team. In Puerto Rico, where we celebrated a quarter century of doing business this year, we have, for example, one of the best maintenance men God ever installed on this planet. He can mend a precision timepiece with the same ease that he can repair a 500-ton injection moulding machine. Above all, what he has is common sense. His name is José Ramon Garcia, but we've taken to calling him Dominic, because he hails from the Dominican Republic.

A hurricane once blew the roof off our warehouse in Puerto Rico. A senior manager told me not to worry, even though we had $3 million in telecommunications inventory and work-in-progress sitting in storage. 'Just rain water,' he said. On the advice of Dominic, I called the manager and asked him to dip his forefinger in the 'rain water' that was on top of one of the thinly covered loads of electronics, and taste it. 'Salt water,' he said with astonishment. 'Hurricane rainwater always is,' I responded. Without Dominic's warning, we could have shipped damaged merchandise to customers and lost out on what proved to be a $2 million + insurance claim. This is the same Dominic who some time later would wrestle the winds to the ground and protect our inventory during a subsequent hurricane. He parked two large trucks loaded with ballast on either side of the warehouse and then stretched steel cables over the roof of the warehouse, attached to the trucks on either end. Surprised insurance executives taking photos of this extraordinary tactic were invited to breakfast with us. Common sense, isn't it? It wasn't so common before everybody started doing it.

My most endearing memory of Dominic relates to something that happened one wintry Sunday morning in Stockholm. In a quickly made deal, we had just bought L.M. Ericsson's surge-arrestor business. We were invited to visit Ericsson on Monday and arrange the final details of the transfer. Dominic, a lean and handsome man with a proud, poised manner, walked into the conference room in a white tropical suit with a carnation in his buttonhole. Word of the meeting reached him just as he was to walk his first daughter down the aisle, but he saw the importance of the meeting and caught the next flight from San Juan to be in Stockholm on Sunday so we could prepare properly. I told him this was above and beyond the call of duty. He shook his head and said, 'This is my job and where I belong. We — all of us in our factory — owe our rice and beans to this business.'

Dominic has done the right thing again and again, and his boldest achievement was probably the following. We use an extremely powerful, custom-designed 500-ton press to mould precision plastic housings for our surge protectors. The drive shaft that powers this press is fourteen inches in diameter. It cracked. With that baby out of commission, we stood to lose an entire $50 million order from one of our biggest customers. Immediately we searched everywhere to get it fixed. We even had the moulds for the shaft to re-cast it. Everyone said that it would cost us three to five times as much to repair the shaft as to buy a new press. And the time to fix it? It might take six months. What if we used double time? It would still take three months. And, if we bought a new press? A custom-made press would take just about as long to deliver. In that case, we were out of business.

Dominic came into my office and said, 'Mr Roach, we have a holiday on Friday. Let me and my special maintenance crew work over the weekend.' What did I have to lose? They welded the mould and hand-smoothed the join with oiled emery cloths so it shone and felt like glass. They had fixed it. Their hands had to be raw from the work.

I wanted to bonus Dominic and his people for this extraordinary effort and told them so. He pleaded with me not to. 'This will destroy the people I work with,' he said. 'This is our company, too.' Because of pride of ownership, they would not take a bonus, and they were nearly defiant about their resolve. You can get emotional about people like that.

I have always advocated energised workplaces, especially in the Caribbean; and I like it that way. When *First Blood* — the initial Rambo movie — came out in 1982, I decided to liven up the factory on one of my regular visits; so I dressed up like a Green Beret — open-shirted, with criss-crossed munition belts, a kerchief around my head, a big cigar drooping out of my mouth, and waving an unloaded automatic rifle. When I barged onto the shop floor, the front-office people streamed in and thought it was an insurrection. In a way, it was — an insurrection of the spirit; the workers loved it.

Imitating Sylvester Stallone is not the customary behaviour of a 67-year-old CEO, who was regularly visiting the White House and chairing committees for the International

Policy Forum. But I didn't care; the people loved it. Still today, I'll walk into that plant, and gradually a drumming will start up, very softly at first, and then growing almost deafening as they — especially the *señoras* and *señoritas* — chant and pound: *Rambo regresó! Rambo regresó!* — 'Rambo's Back!'

The workers on the assembly line and I have forged a real pact, and nowhere is that pact more evident than in matters of quality control. The 'eyes' on the line are the real quality inspectors.

Seven hundred parts would be moving down the assembly line at a pretty good clip. I could nab one and then a minute later grab another. Each would have a tiny imperfection. Charlie Roberts, our retired manufacturing guru and a pivotal figure in the founding of TII, would be baffled and scratch his head, 'How in hell did you do that?' These problems were as new to Charlie as they were to me. In the end, I had to reveal my secret to him. The women on the line would nod towards the defects with their eyes. I was just obeying their commands. They were tipping me off to cosmetic things that a supervisor might ignore. Someone was simply trying to get products out the door. 'Just forget it,' the worker's line supervisor would say. 'It has nothing to do with the electrical properties of the product.'

Watching the eyes of workers on the line is something I have tried to train each of our managers to do, and the payoff has been terrific. Feargal Quinn, one of Ireland's leading managers, has written, 'You are not listening to customers at all if someone else does your listening for you.'* When it comes to quality control, the same is true: No management team should feel it is doing the quality control job unless the team members are personally involved in it.

---

*   Quinn, Feargal, *Crowning the Customer: How to Become Customer-Driven*. Dublin: O'Brien Press, 1990, p. 70.

It's lunch time, and one group of our employees scurries from the assembly line to the cafeteria and dining-room our management has built for the workers. Some line up for the rice and Caribbean chicken on the menu today. The smell is succulent. Others run up to hug youngsters bringing their *madré* a steaming canister of black-bean soup. One woman makes a point of stopping and telling me, in English that she has rehearsed with great care, how much the plant has meant to her life and that it is cleaner than her kitchen floor — news that leaves me beaming with pride. Our conversation is interrupted, however, by an insistent young man tugging at her skirt. I judge him to be about seven, he holds a food canister to which he points hungrily, and his message is clear: *'¡Quiero esto! Mamá, por favor, quiero esto!'* — 'I want some of that. Mamma, please, I want some of that!' The *niño's* urgent plea and the passion in his gaze bring a tear to my eye and a powerful memory to my mind.

1

Setting the Table (1922–31)

Al Roach was born in a cold-water flat in Harlem in 1915. His father worked first on the New York docks and then in a shop that blended and sold edible oils. His mother, who bore ten children, was a decisive influence on Al's childhood and dealt with his stubborn and independent spirit through a combination of discipline and encouragement. The family moved to newly developing Brooklyn when Al was eight, part of an ethnic mass migration to the New York suburbs by Irish-Americans.

In school, Dominican nuns were strict teachers, but they also encouraged Al's sense of humanity and fair play. Even before his family left Harlem, Al demonstrated entrepreneurial behaviour by staging fist fights in front of elevated train stops where cheering onlookers pitched coins. In Brooklyn, ten-year-old Al organised other youngsters to move and sell top-soil. Without guidance, he displayed the natural instincts of a manager. Among his brothers and sisters, though not the eldest, he was still the leader.

As the second son, Al seemed destined for the seminary, but a series of authority conflicts with priests made him reconsider that path. The tension was augmented by an incident relating to a particularly successful campaign to raise food for the needy before the Thanksgiving Day holiday, spearheaded by Al and the football team to which he belonged.

When the Great Depression descended, Al's father took a considerable pay cut. The older children left school and found jobs wherever they could. For Al, that meant work at a greengrocer, where much of the pay was in over-ripe and bruised fruits and vegetables. Convinced his family would be better off without his meagre income than with him to feed and lodge, Al hopped a freight in 1931 and joined the legions of homeless roving through America during this time of economic collapse. His formal education having ended, he had no special work skills to offer besides determination ... and the fists and footwork of a street-wise kid.

'I w-a-n-t *that*! Mom, tell me what I have to do to get *t-h-a-t*!'

Gazing through the frost-glazed living-room window of our cold-water tenement in Harlem, my seven-year-old eyes were riveted to the dining-car of the New York Central Twentieth Century Limited. The Limited had just pulled out of the Park Avenue Tunnel from Grand Central rolling westward to Chicago, and lingered for a moment on the tracks in front of our home as it sometimes did.

My children, grandchildren, and great-grand-children have all played with electric trains as they scampered on thick pile carpets in suburban living rooms. I had it better. The train of my youth and of my dreams was real. Its jet-black steam locomotive driven by a 5,000-horsepower engine, followed by a string of dark green Pullman cars, and pausing just 50 feet away. Mogul Cornelius Vanderbilt, one of the wealthiest men in all New York, might own it, but I wanted a piece of the action. I wanted a seat at that table.

In the twilight, the dining-car glistened with glasses and goblets. Why so many of them? What were they all for? Flickering candles. Silver flatware. Floral centre-pieces. Why do they put bed sheets on the tables? I wondered. Waiters in white coats were weaving through the aisle, balancing trays capped by sparkling silver domes. My three-year-old sister Margaret, with eyes big as saucers, tugged at my shirt and asked repeatedly, 'What are they eating?' I scarcely knew, but it had to be good, and I wanted my helping. How would I get it? 'Education, Alfred. A narrowback has nothin' at all to be ashamed of,' my mother Nellie answered.

Why do mothers speak in riddles, especially when you're seven? What could a seat at the table have to do with the width of my back? Years later, the message sank in. I understood that broadbacks in the tragic tradition of our Irish ancestors, survived by their brawn, if they survived at all. Use your head, she meant. Forget the ditches and the docks. Find a desk. Or, as I put it today: mobilise your *brainpower*!

That question was the start of *me*. And, it is a question that has demanded ever-fresh answers. That dining-car wasn't just luxury — it was *moving*. In the coming years, I learned that getting a seat at the table was one thing. *Keeping* it was quite another. That demanded daily disciplines, such as patience, perseverance, and preparation.

But I get ahead of myself. The aroma of real food steaming from the cast-iron stove in our crowded kitchen put an end to my reverie that night seventy-six years ago. Stuffed fresh ham, sauerkraut and mashed potatoes laden in the familiar chipped crockery on the faded red-and-white oilcloth-covered table: it seemed good enough for then, and its savoury memory still entices me today.

I was born in this flat on 119th Street and Park Avenue, above the pet shop Mrs Cannell owned. Park Avenue is one of the richest stretches in all of Manhattan, except when it reaches Harlem. There it's called the Park Avenue of the Poor. I was child number three. There were to be ten of us. It was an exciting time to be alive — restless and full of extremes. In 1922, Prohibition had entered its second year. Business at the speakeasy down the street was booming.

Before Prohibition, my grandfather Roach was a publican and owned a string of as many as six taverns (the number climbed to sixteen as my father grew older). Grandad had an acid test for hiring a bartender. He would ask 'Now, my good man, I would like a straight answer to a simple question: how much do you steal?'

If the guy said, 'God, Mr Roach, I'd never do that,' it was 'So long, buster.' But if the candidate said, 'That depends on what you pay me', he had a reasonable chance of a job.

The old man made his bartenders wear vests and aprons without pockets to keep the stealing down. When the bar was real busy one day, the barrel went dry and he had to run downstairs himself to pull up another keg to tap. While downstairs, Grandfather heard this mysterious clinking coming from the other side of the basement floor. That night he closed up himself and then snooped around the floor on the level below. He found a large pickle jar filled with coins. A broad tin tube sat in the jar and extended all the way up to the basement ceiling. When he went back upstairs, he found that someone had cut a slot in the top of the bar and a hole in the main floor. One of the bartenders was sneaking coins through the slot to his secret cache in the basement. Grandad emptied the coins from the jar and put a rat trap in instead. The next night a bartender went down to the cellar, supposedly to tap a keg. Moments later, everyone heard a bellowing yell from below. I was very young when I learned the real lesson of the story. My grandfather and his bartenders wasted a lot of time trying to outsmart each other. In the end, Grandad sold the taverns.

'Why not think big and share big instead?'

My father understood the world better than my grandfather. My dad taught me the principle of barter. After working on the docks as a longshoreman, he got a job in a naval store, about a block away from the piers. The shop sold edible and scented oils that it custom blended. The mark-up was huge. The place also carried linseed oil, and that naturally put Dad into the paint business. If you needed paint at a particular price ... like free ... you could come up with six pounds of sturgeon or salmon — things average people could never afford to buy.

What happened when the salmon appeared? Even a family with nine children (one died shortly after birth) couldn't chow down six pounds of salmon, and we had no refrigerator. It was too much fish for one family, so Dad visited neighbours and traded part of the catch for a crate of apples or a sack of potatoes. Sometimes a case of crackers would 'fall off a truck' and miraculously never touch the ground. It would end up in the stream of bartered goods. Sure, part of it was outright theft, and no one could condone it today. But the rules were different then. Workers were exploited more, and they got back at the owners with a little creativity. Watching my father taught me the art of cutting deals, and the importance of looking out for the other guy's self-interest.

Harlem was getting tougher. One Sunday morning, one of my sisters went down to the local drugstore to buy my dad a paper. From the window, my dad could see that a man was trying to molest her. Dad jumped out the window to the ground nearly fifteen feet below and nearly beat the living daylights out of the pervert. Not long afterwards, a speeding truck driver crushed a two-year-old down the street. 'Enough is enough, Nellie,' my father said. 'We can afford our own home and our yard where the kids can play.' We were not alone. We became part of the great migration for the Irish and other groups to suburbs like the fringe areas of Brooklyn.

In November 1923, when I was eight, we left Harlem for Gerritsen Beach in the Sheepshead Bay area of Brooklyn, sitting on reclaimed marsh land. A $3,000 bungalow with a basement, kitchen, dining-room, porch, three bedrooms and, most importantly, our own bathroom. No more trips into a cold tenement loo, shared with other families.

When we moved into Gerritsen Beach, developers were still building and digging up fine black top-soil in piles. I was an ambitious youngster and a strong one — my muscles had started to bulge from shovelling coal into the family furnace, and I must have been no more than ten years old. People wanted that top-soil to landscape their new lots, and I was determined to find a way to get it to them. I started out hauling top-soil in an abandoned baby carriage at a dime a basket. Then I learned that I could get $3 for a load of top-soil and that I could rent a horse and cart for $3. One Saturday, I did ten loads and, gosh, was I tired, but I made a profit of $27! The next Saturday I hired a couple of guys, but got a larger cart with two horses, which cost $5. They did the work; I did the marketing; and we sold it at four bucks a load. We sold ten loads for $40, and I gave each of them $6. They thought it was fantastic. Being $23 richer after paying for the cart and the wages, and not nearly as sore, so did I! In those days, a common labourer was lucky to make $15–$20 a week.

The Horse Before the Cart, The Heart Before the Horse

As I manage more and more enterprises, the value of empathy strikes home with me as never before. What does the other guy want? What does the other guy need? Find that answer and respond to it in a focused way, and you have unleashed immeasurable energy on your behalf.

No matter how hard you work, you personally can work only 18 to 20 hours a day, and you can't keep that pace up for very long. Learn to manage people, and you get a terrific multiple on what you do. You've heard the old saying: 'It's not how hard you work, but how smart you work.' Forget you and your wants! The real issue is how smart you can get the people around you to work with you. To inspire people to work smart, they must feel respected. I could have paid my buddies far less, and they would have been happy. At $6 a day, they were ecstatic and worked like it. You have to put your heart to work first to get the horse before the cart and to keep him moving at a good clip.

There were great temptations to be aggressive, to barter, to make deals. A guy could easily end up drifting the wrong way. Two forces helped steer me straight: the nuns at school and my mother at home.

At Resurrection School, my academic grades were good, but my marks for conduct were a chronicle of catastrophe. I was always headed for mischief or determined to be the class clown. The Dominican nuns had a great influence keeping me on the right road. School was as much a moral force as an educational one for me.

When I was ten or eleven, the Brooklyn parochial school system had just introduced the idea of a parent-teacher conference. My mother went up to the first one about me, and the nun told her 'Mrs Roach, he will never be mediocre. He will either be President or the greatest gangster in the country.'

My mother was a lady and, of course, she wouldn't get emotional in front of the sister. But as soon as she walked in our front door, you could actually hear her left hand whiz through the air headed for my right cheek.

Stunned, I yelled out, 'What did you hit me for?'

'Sister Florita said you're going to become a gangster.'

'But, what about President? She said I might be President, too.'

'Well, I didn't hit you for that ... only the other one ... and, you keep that in mind, Alfred.'

When I was twelve, Sr Florita actually kept me back an entire school year. My ego stung, but to this day, I remember her with the most warmth of any of these Dominican nuns. Those nuns could mete out their own punishment, and they had a weapon of choice. It was a three-cornered ruler, and they would crack you with it over the knuckles. You remembered that, I'll tell you!

In the fourth grade, we had a nun — Sr Gabriel — who used to wind up before she delivered, almost like the American baseball pitcher Satchel Paige. One day I saw her go into the stretch right beside my desk, and, in my mind, I could see my fingers snapping like pieces of chalk. I waited till the last second and than jerked my hand away. She missed me. She missed the desk. But she managed to club herself right in the shins, and did she scream!

One wiseguy in class went home and told his mother that Al Roach hit the nun. When the neighbourhood telegraph reached my mother, she didn't even ask for an explanation. I got the hell beaten out of me. So, I went back and told Sr Gabriel that somebody said I hit her and my mother smacked me around for it. She said, 'That's so wrong.' She called my mother up and told her that it was absolutely false. Even better, she lectured the class and said, 'Whoever did that has committed a mortal sin and had better go to confession. It's a terrible lie. The fault was mine. I missed his hand.'

She had them all going to hell, and I was the martyr — which I played to the hilt. Over two days, from sinner to saint. At the ten o'clock break, she invited me over to the convent for cookies and milk.

Being bounced from nuns to mother and mother to nuns kept me in line. 'I'll *mass-a-crate* you,' my mother used to say. My mother was investigator, marshal, judge, jury, and executioner, all rolled into one. She punished decisively and on the spot. I think parents today lack that kind of decisiveness, which is still needed, even though physical punishment for children is no longer appropriate. My mother never left any unfinished business for my father. She threatened to cut the gizzard out of us when we crossed the line. We never pressed to find out what that meant. None of us kids in trouble ever wanted to get Dad involved. We were always warned that if he got into the act, it would be awful beyond belief. In fact, he never did anything. It was a big bluff. 'If I ever tell your father that you did that, he'll break both of your...' That generally was enough. Both what? We could only guess.

I wasn't the only one to run foul of her. My eldest brother Eddie saw my mother pregnant with my youngest brother Herbie and said, 'Ma, not again.'

She landed a slap straight on his face, armed with wedding ring and all. 'What if I thought that about you, you wouldn't be here,' she shouted. 'See all those stars up there. Those are babies yet to come.'

Stay right where you are, I thought not a few years later. Just keep shining.

From my father, I learned ingenuity and diligence. But my Mom, not my father, ran the family in nearly every respect. She dominated. Was it her physical force and dominance that mattered most to me? No. In truth, she used her power sparingly. It was really her gentleness and intellect that I remember most.

My mother had great spirit. I will never forget the scent of lavender she deeply favoured. I would experience it when I brushed her indigo-black hair. Her hair was beautiful. Her brain was better. She could always break down a complex problem with her tenacious intellect, and, if not, she would route it to God or a particular saint. Certainly she would have wanted to have children, but not ten of them. Nellie would have gone to college. She would have been a computer wiz. No doubt, she would have been a scientist or a doctor if she were alive and forty today.

My mother helped shape my goals and was probably the single most influential person in my life. The nuns gave me discipline and had my deep respect, but the priests were a different matter. With them, I had run-ins.

I was one of two boys picked to go away to Cathedral College high school, which was really part of a seminary. Although the training was to equip you for the priest-hood, no more than 5 or 10 per cent of the students ended up ordained. But, the education was terrific.

I was talked out of it by a priest — Fr Buckley —who was trying to be funny, but I took him seriously. He said, 'Alfred, I hear tell you're going to become a priest. Well, I don't think you'll be a priest long. I think they'll make you a bishop. You have the makings of a good bishop, but you realise of course that they castrate you, don't you?'

I thought he meant circumcised, and I said I already was.

'Well,' he said, 'that's fine, then you won't be having any problems at all.'

Finally, I asked some of the big guys what castration meant. They asked why I wanted to know, and I said that's what Fr Buckley said happens when you become a priest. One guy opened his eyes wide, and explained it.

'Forget it,' I told my mother, but I didn't tell her why. 'Go,' she advised. 'Go, if only for a couple of years.'

No way — I didn't know when they were going to perform the act — if they'd catch me sleeping or what.

I was the second eldest son, and although some thought I was destined for the priesthood, I knew that the collar wasn't for me. (Actually it was my sister Margaret who took vows — and who has been a remarkable and effective Dominican teacher for over a half century.) The fire inside me was growing — a restlessness to find my seat at that elusive table of success — but I didn't know how it would happen. The world around me had a tough though appealing order to it, but shortly after my fourteenth birthday, we would all be affected by an event of massive proportions — the Great Depression — and it launched the beginning of my journey.

In the New York of the 1920s, I can remember the chauffeured limousines, waiting for the big bosses to descend from the office buildings. America worshipped at the temple of Wall Street. No one bought a stock outright. It was a boom built on margin. In October 1929, pop went the bubble.

The shop my father was a foreman in was on Front and John Streets — near the insurance district. The day after the stock market crashed, I told him I would be coming to see him, and he warned me to be careful: 'Whatever you do, when you get into that goddamn Wall Street, stay in close to those goddamn buildings, because those goddamn idiots think they can fly.'

During the Depression, money just disappeared. It vanished. Jobs were gone. Savings evaporated. My parents had eighty bucks in the bank, and they lost every cent. Afterwards, they kept their money in mattresses like everyone else. All of a sudden, average people and the poor felt the impact.

In our family's Brooklyn bungalow, I was on familiar terms with our great, big coal-burning furnace in the basement, having stoked it for five years. We kids thought central heating, unknown in Harlem, a great luxury. It was also the communications centre for learning the family secrets. There were furnace gratings throughout the house for the heat to come up. They were our listening posts as the voices of our parents filtered through the system.

Some things you didn't want to hear, but you needed to. Not long after the crash, my father came home one day looking tired and stricken. 'You lost your job, didn't you?' my mother asked nervously.

'I didn't lose my job, Nellie, but the boss gave me a helluva cut. He took me from $65 to $18 a week.' He sat down in the living-room, totally demoralised.

That was less than $1,000 a year. The mortgage on the house was $20 a month. We kids talked among ourselves. My elder sister Helen was in her junior year of high school. She dropped out and went to work at the phone company. I was fourteen, with a part-time job in a vegetable market. I dropped out of school and went to work full time, earning about $8 a week.

Education. Being a narrowback. Nice thoughts, but not for now.

Part of my deal with the owner of the produce store was to get, in addition to my weekly wage, a couple of bags of vegetables and fruits that were turning. It helped the family. And I always made sure that the bruised apples, the wilting lettuce, and the brown bananas were on the top of the bags I carried out of the store. The stuff below might not have been *all that* ripe. Would I do it today? Not on your life. But then was then, and times were tough. We never went hungry — not so much because of what I did, but because we all chipped in.

I began to see myself as a manager and enjoyed getting people together to make things happen. I organised a football team called the Gerritsen Beach Huskies. It was one of the best-known amateur football teams in all of New York. We bought our own uniforms — blue and white with gold helmets. With a usual 'donation' of a quarter a head dropped into our 'collection basket' helmet, we used to play to crowds of 200 on a vacant lot across from Resurrection Church on Sunday after mass.

Fifteen years old, I was now number-one altar boy at Resurrection Church and general manager of the football team. At the end of the season, the Huskies had $350 in the kitty, left over from the collections we made. What were we going to do with it? This was in the Depression in 1930. Someone said, 'Let's give out Thanksgiving baskets.'

I thought that was great, but then someone said, 'How many can you give out? Maybe thirty or forty.' But, hundreds of people needed help. We dug in. We went around to the churches to find out who needed help the most.

The Catholic Church was the biggest. The neighbourhood was 70 per cent Catholic — mostly Irish. There were also a lot of Germans and Norwegians, who were Lutheran. There was even a little synagogue with a congregation of about twenty. The Lutheran pastor was surprised and elated when we visited his home. He called to his wife and said 'Gwendoline, come down here and look at this. Here's an altar boy from the Church of the Resurrection and he wants the addresses of our neediest.'

Enter an old Irish priest, Fr Cox (rest his soul) down at Resurrection. He'd like his nip; I know it because I used to get it for him down at O'Dwyer's Saloon. This was during Prohibition. He said it was for his cough ... or for his asthma. Maybe both.

Father Cox didn't go for my football kitty charity. He reminded me that the Church had a St Vincent de Paul Society for that. 'You just give us the money that you have, and we'll take care of it,' he advised.

'No,' I argued. 'It's not my money. We have Protestants and Jews on our team, too.' I refused to hand it over.

This was a truly breakthrough campaign. Instead of forty baskets, we ended up with three hundred and fifty — big bushel baskets with hams in them, and cabbages, potatoes, turnips and canned foods, the latter contributed by people in the neighbourhood. The fathers of a couple of the fellows were in the moving business, and they lent us the trucks. We had uniformed cheerleaders and record players blaring out the Notre Dame fight song and the Washington Huskie song, and we collected three vans full of canned goods.

The next week at eleven o'clock mass, which Fr Cox knew my mother regularly attended, he landed on me in his sermon with all the sweetness of his Gaelic brogue. His sermon went something like this: 'We have a little lad here. You know him, because he has a football moustache ... eleven hairs on each side. Now, he wants to take it upon himself to do the work of the St Vincent de Paul Society. I like the young man. I know his mother is here this morning in the congregation ... and he'd be mightily helped — I think — by a word of direction from his parents.

Some think he may be dancing on the edge of *ex-com....*'

You could actually hear the gasps in the pews. 'Well, no,' the crafty Fr Cox went on, knowing that he had just targeted my mother with the pressure of every God-fearing Catholic. 'I think it's better that I should speak directly with his mother after mass.' That did it. Fr Cox told Mom that her wee Alfred might be *'ex-com-moon-ee-cated'* (as he put it) if he didn't stop this nonsense. I'm not sure that she knew what that meant, but it sounded too damned close to 'execution' for my own good. When I got home, I tried to explain the principle to my mother, but she just shook her head, frowning.

The Huskies were important to me, but it was just a football team. My job at the fruit and vegetable market helped out a little, but I felt as though I was more of a drain on the family than an asset. If I left, I reasoned, there might be more for the others. Above all, I was restless.

One day, I just hopped a freight — the Nickel Plate Line — chugging west to Buffalo.

No waiters in white, no crystal goblets, no sparkling silver. A dusty, rattling box car with its entourage of hobos and uprooted families. I remember a woman in a tattered plaid dress cradling a baby in one arm and a battered enamel pot in the other. Here I was — fifteen years old, a high-school dropout, jobless, and without the hint of a goal or a destination. Mother of God, what kind of table was I setting for myself?

2

Battling Al (1931–36)

Still not 16, Al tasted life in the 'jungle' of freight trains and makeshift camps, dodging private railroad cops and begging door-to-door ... even the safe haven of a night in jail to elude molesters and paedophiles. Rather than focusing on the despair, he was amazed at the kindness human beings were able to show towards each other in adversity.

In 1933, after several aimless journeys west and back to Brooklyn, Al joined the army and was stationed on Corregidor, a strategically important island near the Philippines. In the army, he found his first true opportunity to be recognised as exceptional. In 1935 and 1936, he won the Army–Navy Welterweight Boxing Championship for the Philippines.

General Douglas MacArthur, later American Pacific Theater commander during the Second World War, was both US Army commander in the Philippines and a military advisor to the Philippine nation. A passionate sports fan, he took a liking to young Al. Not enthused about a personal service job, Al declined to become MacArthur's driver. Instead he pursued the lucrative 'perquisite' awarded the boxing champion — overseeing base gambling operations. After a while, Al was earning as much as $2,000 a month ... on top of his $18 monthly wages as an army private. At the time, MacArthur himself earned only $9,000 a year!

Al's meteoric success in the ring made him consider becoming a professional. His hopes of competing for the Philippines in the 1936 Berlin Olympics, were dashed when the International Olympic Committee ruled that his US citizenship barred him from representing the Philippines.

Returning to the US, when his tour of duty ended in the summer of 1936, Al still considered professional boxing a possible career. To test how good he really was, he agreed to an informal match-up in the ring of Stillman's Gym with a seemingly sluggish and overweight adversary.

'Who the hell stole me beautiful boots?'

I remember screaming that question as I woke up in the Peoria jailhouse, and the greatest pair of hiking boots I had ever owned was gone. The night before, exhausted, I had set them by my cot after I had pried them off. Instead of my handsome, sturdy Sears Roebuck hiking boots, there stood the sorriest, rottenest pair of old shoes I had ever seen, covered with paint, mud and gunk. Worst of all, these gunboats were two *sizes* too big for me! The guy who stole mine must have snipped the toes off to fit in ... or maybe traded them with a fellow traveller.

There's no record, I'm sure, of an Al Roach being in jail in Peoria or anywhere else. The cops — the decent ones, at least — would round up kids like myself on the road and lock us up for the night to keep us out of the reach of paedophiles and perverts (but not, as I learned, out of the clutches of shoe-rustlers). 'Give me *a* name,' the desk sergeant would bark when he booked you for the night. *A* name — not *your* name. I soon got my string of aliases like 'Andy Regan' and 'Artie Russell'. In the morning, they usually fed you some sort of breakfast before you were let loose — gruel or dried bread and lard, but some days it was all your belly saw. Not much to keep the fire stoked for a fifteen-year-old ... or for anyone else.

What do the people who experienced the Great Depression most remember about it? Some say it was the hopeless poverty or the degradation. But there's no doubt about my personal answer. For me, it was the unexpected acts of kindness shown by one compassionate human being towards another in need. No *maître d*'s to relieve the relentless hunger on these freight trains criss-crossing America, but the locomotive engineers were often unsung heroes. They would purposely brake long and slow before entering certain towns where the cops were thugs who relished beating up indigents. It gave the human cargo a chance to vault from the moving train without snapping an arm or spraining an ankle.

My most memorable Depression heroine was in Ohio. I went into a diner in Toledo. Generally the counter waitresses would chase us out: 'We don't serve your kind. Get outta here, you bum, before I call the cops.'

I went into this diner off Emerald Avenue near the Maumee River with just 25 cents and ordered a cup of soup and coffee from a red-headed gal. Her hair was pulled back tight in a bun and her green X-ray eyes could have pierced lead. Next thing I knew, along came a big bowl of tomato soup, a juicy hamburger smothered with all the trimmings, and a big piece of peach pie à la mode. I was scared to death. 'I didn't order that,' I gulped. 'I only ordered soup.'

'I have your money,' the waitress answered with the ramrod backbone of a Marine drill sergeant. 'Eat what's in front of you, shut your mouth, and here's your change.' Two quarters, she gave me back.

Any time I go into a diner today, and I see an overworked waitress, the tip she gets is twice the cost of what I ate and often a twenty to boot. Ms Toledo Drill Sergeant with the Big Heart, I still see your gorgeous face today....

After about a week on the road, I met a master. He was all of 16, but his frail moustache was twice as thick as mine and he knew *all* the tricks. To get food, I would jump off the freights and knock on doors, offering to do work — clean the yard or do this and that. They'd set the dog on me.

'Wrong technique, buddy,' my new friend says, shaking his head mournfully. He gets some coal dust and tells me to wet my finger, then he shows me how to put damp streaks on my face. 'When you hear them opening the door, make your bottom lip quiver,' he adds as the next touch. This guy would have put a movie director like John Ford or Frank Capra to shame! 'Try to make your eye water,' he schools me, 'and just quietly say two words: "I-i h-o-o-n-g-r-e-e."'

It was irresistible. Folks always fed you, but they weren't fools. They made you eat the hand-out there. (No technique is perfect.) After a while, I got greedy and wanted them to give me a couple of bags of food to take with me, because sometimes I was already full. I couldn't eat more. I had already hit a couple of houses. Then I learned to say, 'I just got off the train Ma'am, I don't want to dirty your kitchen.'

'How thoughtful,' she would say. 'You stay out here now.'

Sometimes I would stuff my pockets. Other times I wasn't so lucky. The grandmother in her apron would stand on the back porch staring at me sympathetically, with her hands perched on her hips, as I tried to force down yet another bite of a bologna and pickle sandwich.

After an episode in Butte, Montana, I saw this routine was going nowhere. Without a place to sleep and the rain streaming down in sheets, the guy at the desk of the Salvation Army asked me, 'Where you from, son?'

'New York,' I said.

'We're full up. I guess you'd better go back to New York.'

It was then I learned never to say I was a New Yorker when I was on the road. New Jersey, Connecticut — that's OK, and it explained the accent, but never New York. Most of America had this thing about New Yorkers, at least back then.

The visit also scarred me in another way. For the longest time I would never contribute to the Salvation Army. They do great work. But not for me when I needed it, and remembered it. What a concerned cop, a locomotive eer, or a gold-hearted waitress — each acting on vn — could do for other people who needed help, d institutions would sometimes fail at miserably.

ad, I learned I really *was* tough, and I *talked* crazy, but I wasn't afraid of a thing. The ss of my journey bothered me, not the dan- the time, the United States seemed balkanised — the Oakies were like the outcasts of the former Yugoslavia. It took the strong leadership of a man like Franklin Roosevelt to equip people with a purpose and to give many back their dignity.

After a couple of months of riding rails, I longed for the sights, smells, sounds, and tastes of Brooklyn. And suddenly I felt I was back at the Coney Island amusement park in Brooklyn.

Our whole family has piled into the city bus for a nickel, and then taken the train for another five cents. As usual, the ticket-taker 'forgets' to count all the kids. His Coleman moustache goes up with his upper lip as he passes the verdict, 'Eight kids? Buddy, you got four, as I see it....'

My brother Jim gives me a playful whack as we push through the turnstile, and I jab back at him. I see my sister Annie's hazel eyes and the flash of her beautiful auburn hair in the afternoon sun. It glows like the coat of a freshly groomed colt. Annie: I was her protector, so much so that she cried on Mom's shoulder that none of the boys would ever come near her let alone touch her.

Then I see myself on *The Cyclone* — the monster roller-coaster. From the deafening screams, we seem headed straight for hell or at least for uncharted parts. It is a precipitous drop. My best girl, Esther, is with me, I am getting the greatest hug of my young life. She is damn near coming through the other side of me! I think I just may pop the question to her tomorrow. I just might.

Then all of us are having lunch at the great open picnic tables. In his mellow, whiskey tenor, Dad is warbling 'A dear little town in the old County Down'. At Coney Island, the brew is Hire's Root Beer in mugs. Nathan's Coney Island Hot Dogs with the works, including sauerkraut and mustard. Clam chowder. Corn on the cob with gobs of butter. I'm the big spender and I pay the tab for all eleven of us, and it's $3.30.

'*Three dollars and t-h-i-r-t-y cents!* Three dollars and thirty cents, you miserable little snoring punk. If you want to ride this train from Scranton to Trenton, it will cost you three dollars and thirty cents, or I suggest you unload your filthy ass off of here ... and I mean, NOW!' The railroad gumshoe also had a Coleman moustache, like the Coney-Island ticket man, but he was thumping a billy club into his left hand, just warming up for my skull and shoulders. I felt sure this was going to hurt a helluva lot more than Sister Gabriel ever could. So, I jumped off the train, realising as I leapt that Coney Island — from Esther's mega-hug to the butter-drenched corn on the cob — was all the afternoon dream of a napping hobo.

My belly knows no fire, only gnawing hunger and loneliness. I want to go home. Go home. But, of course, you can't. Certainly not now.

Still, I returned to Gerritsen Beach, did odd jobs, and crowded back into my brothers' bedroom. 'What are *you* doing back? I thought *you* were gone for good!' Welcome home, Brother.*

There was considerable construction in New York during the early days of the Depression. (In fact, Franklin Roosevelt borrowed some of these same strategies from New York and used them to help turn around the Depression in the US.) Construction jobs could be great, I thought. Guys repairing the subways — eighty bucks a week — but you had to have an in to get a spot, and I didn't. So, I was mostly on the street. Not only was I a tough guy, but I got the reputation for being one, too.

After hopping freights a couple more times and feeling pretty useless at home, I saw an army enlistment poster with a picture of a tropical island and a girl without a bra. And, I decided I had to go there. It was February

---

* The family called me 'Brother' instead of Al because I bore my dad's name.

1933, and so cold. Hedging my bets, I shelled out $10 for an engagement ring for Esther. We would write everyday. On 6 March 1933 I swore my oath to Uncle Sam and I was off. Join the army and see the girls!

The army posted me in Corregidor — a *tiny* island, no bigger than two square miles. Two US bases were ultimately built there, Fort Mills and Kindley Field. Corregidor became part of the Philippines in 1947, but it wasn't yet. Small in size, it had long been mighty in strategic importance. Control Corregidor and you control the gateway to Manila Bay and the Philippines. The first day off the troop carrier, I saw the palm trees begin to shake and heard the earth start to rumble. Gee, I thought, wasn't this a pretty small island to have its own subway system? This New Yorker soon learned he was experiencing his first earthquake, and during the rest of my stay on the island I prayed for a pair of skyhooks to hang onto if the earth beneath me disappeared!

My assignment was to an artillery team responsible for a 12-inch disappearing piece, a cannon about 15 to 20 feet long, with a big shell. For practice firings, we used a shell with enough powder to launch the round, but with no charge to make it explode on impact. Instead, the payload was filled with sand. During one practice firing, our shells kept overshooting the damned target. We needed more ballast, three pounds more we guessed. I suggested, 'Captain, why don't we pour three pounds of water in there.'

A lot of guys laughed. But not for long. The shell landed right on target and I was made Private First Class — the highest form of private in the US Army — then and there. That was probably my first, last, and only contribution to military strategy — having spent most of my life trying to get nations to melt their weapons down, rather than to build them up.

People slaughtering each other on the battlefield was

not my cup of tea, but fighting one-on-one was a very different matter. That was in my blood. It went back a long way to my upbringing, my environment, and maybe even my genes.

My father was blond, blue-eyed, and powerful. He was a short-legged guy and only 5'5", but he commanded a 46-inch barrel chest. Once I saw him lift a 500-pound drum onto a truck with a co-worker. They shimmied the load up between their chests. I shook my head with wonder at how the hell they had been able to do that. It was sheer muscle power. Physically, he was as strong as an ox.

During his late teens (he was born in Greenwich Village in 1888), he boxed an African-American from Mississippi in a bout that earned Dad twelve bucks. When he left the gym, he was unfortunately mugged and lost all his take. That was the end of his professional career. He always said he was sure the promoter arranged both the fight and the mugging.

My first strong recollection of roughhousing is of us as 5- and 6-year-old kids playing 'king of the hill' on snow-piles in Harlem. I'd do *anything* to win, to stay on top of that mound of snow. A normal child would have let others win sometimes. Not me. It's been that way all of my life. While people tell me I've learned to respect the rules with considerable care and to lose with more grace over the years, the fire to be first has never left me.

At the age of seven, I got into a fist-fight on the sidewalk. The other guy was bigger than me and a bit older. The scrap happened about quitting time and men were coming home from work off the Third Avenue El. The next thing I knew, they had gathered around, and they started rooting and throwing pennies and nickels. There were even a few dimes ... and one quarter.

My opponent and I were pals. When the scrap was over, we forgot what started it, and we split the money. I suggested, 'This is a great idea. If there's dough in this, let's stage a scuffle.' So, we did ... and made some more cash.

After a while, I said to myself that this hurt. So, I got two other guys involved, then three or four of them. Pretty soon, I was a promoter — a forerunner of Don King, I might add — and we were putting these fights on all over by the train stops. The fighters divided up one half and I'd take the other half. 'Pay the other guy to take the sock in the mouth, but pay him fairly,' was my motto.

My life as a promoter was short-lived, but the one-to-one combat was not. In places like Harlem, you were in a fight every day. You had to fight back. I couldn't run. Like my dad, my legs were too short. So, I had to learn to fight. Bullies would beat the hell out of a patsy. If you begged 'Please don't hit me', you were dead. If you slugged back hard and fast, they didn't mess with you. You had to walk as though there was a sign hung around your neck:

DON'T TOUCH THIS SONUVABITCH,
I'M CRAZY.

In the army, I found myself back in the fight game, but this time I was determined to do it right. Instead of having it out in parking lots or alleys, I learned to box. In pretty short order, determination and army training made a competitive boxer out of me.

I fought in the welterweight class — the intermediary range between lightweight and middleweight — 135 to 147 pounds. Curly hair, a twenty-eight-inch waist, Kelly-green boxing trunks with a white shamrock. Everyone has their days of grandeur, and those were mine.

Training taught me so many basics, like 'Take care of your legs, and they'll take care of you', because that's where the power and stability of a boxer are to be found. Don't punch from the shoulder, swing deep from the cheek of your butt. I learned that good footwork meant never crossing your left leg with your right. My life-long appreciation of the ballet began with boxing, when I learned that fighters like Georges Carpentier studied ballet techniques to improve their boxing skills. Irish dancer Michael Flatley is also a boxer and the winner of a Golden Gloves title.*

Anyone familiar with the movie *Rocky* knows that Sylvester Stallone's character carried the moniker 'The Italian Stallion'. For the spectators, I was known as 'Battlin' Al Roach', although I must confess that my *nom de guerre* was hardly original. At least two other 'Battling's preceded me. Battling Levinsky won the light heavyweight title in 1916 and Battling Siki beat Georges Carpentier for the title in 1922. Originally I wanted to be known as 'The Fighting Irishman', but I suspected the guys at Notre Dame might hold it against me. The first four decades of this century were the heyday of the Irish in boxing: Kid McCoy, Philadelphia Jack O'Brien, Mike McTigue, and Jack Dempsey, who was part Irish and part Indian and was known as 'The Manassa Mauler', because he hailed from Manassa, Colorado.

Then came the Welterweight Championship fight in the Philippines. It was for a dual crown for both the army and navy. I made a mistake in sizing up my opponent. Having out-boxed him time after time in gym sparring matches, I was overconfident and trained for the bout casually. It wasn't until I was in the ring that I changed my attitude. In seconds after the championship match began, I knew I was in trouble. Taking what he was dishing out was tough. It was remembering that the other guy could be tired too that enabled me to win. I could beat him, but I had to work — *I had to make him tired.* Fighters will tell you how hard it is to come back when you are tired and hurt. But, it's that very thing that makes the difference. My opponent went down in the sixth round. I

---

*   Garavan, T.N. et al., *Entrepreneurship & Business Start-Ups in Ireland. Volume 2: Cases.* Dublin: Oak Tree Press, 1997, p. 57.

won the title in both 1935 and 1936. What mattered to me was the lesson the whole experience taught me about the power of preparation and about self-determination. The trophy with the inscription: 'Welterweight Champion of the United States Army, Philippine Department 1935–1936' occupies a proud place on my mantel to this day.

How Negotiating is Like Prize-Fighting

No experience in my early life helped me to become a better business negotiator than my boxing days in the Philippines. Here's how the skills are alike:

- Both reward toughness, but not rigidity

- Both demand first-class training

- Both value preparation over instinct

- Both require exact study of the opponent

- Both practise the art of timing

- Both esteem stamina over flash

- Both are won more often by TKOs* than KOs.

As to the event itself, this I do remember: out of the steamy haze surrounding the outdoor ring, a figure of incomparable bearing and confidence strode forward when it was over. I had heard that he was at every boxing

---

* A technical knockout is a decision awarded by ringside judges based on skill in the ring when a bout is not determined by knocking an opponent out.

match, and there he was in the flesh. It was General Douglas MacArthur. The General loved boxing, and I had heard that he might be there. He was wearing an open-neck shirt with brilliant stars on his collar and an officer's hat splattered with 'scrambled eggs' — considerable golden decoration — on his general's hat. 'That's the kind of courage that will keep us on top. You're the kind of man we want. You didn't quit!' he said in his deep, gravelly voice as he pounded me on the back.

As superintendent at West Point in the early 1920s, MacArthur did a lot to beef up the athletic programme there. He was also head of the US Olympic Committee in 1928, before becoming Army Chief of Staff. In 1935, MacArthur was simultaneously a general in the US Army and a senior military advisor to the Philippines. He had been appointed Field Marshal of the Philippine Army by Manuel Quezon, then Philippine President (whom I also got to know). In 1937, a year after I left the Philippines, MacArthur retired from the US Army to develop the fighting forces of the Philippines, but he was brought back by the US in the Second World War. MacArthur wanted me as a driver in 1935, but I said I wasn't a good driver. The truth was I had too much goddamn pride in me to be anything like a valet. The legendary corncob pipe? I never saw MacArthur smoke one until the Second World War.

Although not his driver, I still got to spend some time around the General. One trick I learned from him was to fall asleep, if only for a few minutes, when you have nothing else to do. When there was nothing happening in the car or at his desk, he would fall asleep and awake truly refreshed, batteries recharged.

Becoming a boxing champ brought about a funny change: it made me really pull back from engaging in personal fights. When I went to a bar, there would always be some guy wanting to take a swing at me. All of a sudden, my peripheral vision would note a fist coming at me. The guy wanted to be known as, 'I knocked out Al Roach, Welter-weight Champion.' Prize fighters — Jack Dempsey, Mike Tyson, you name them — always did and still do travel with bodyguards. When you've earned money with your fists, they become dangerous weapons under the law in New York.

Pick When to Pick a Fight

There's a time to stand up and a time when you didn't hear. My grandmother used to say, God gave you two ears and one mouth, so you'd only talk half as much as you listen. Let it go. Especially, if your spouse has said something they didn't mean to. Don't escalate the situation with: 'What did you say?' It's better to have your better part come back with, 'You never pay attention to me,' than getting into a championship brawl. The older you get, the more valuable you learn time to be.

And, as to those South Sea Island beauties without bras? Well, I got to know the head of customs in the Philippines, and I went to his home often for dinner and learned the native Tagalog language from the Jesuits. Especially one phrase — *'Oh, beautiful maiden'*. (I've learned the key phrases in various languages — Swahili, Chinese, whatever. I learn 'How is your family?' and hope they reply 'Well', because if they say something else, I'm in the ditch.)

The customs director's daughter was dazzling. (I never saw her without a bra, I might add.) When I left the Islands, the director had a tear in his eye. He was probably in his late forties, but then he looked to me like an old man. He said, 'You will probably meet many people, Alfred, but you will never meet people who love you more than we do. The only thing that lifts our spirits is your promise that you will come back.' For me, the Philippine Islands hold gracious memories.

Esther had vanished from my horizon. Her *Dear Alfred* letter had arrived and explained how the pain of waiting was unendurable. I shrugged it off — she probably got tired of cleaning the tarnish off a ten-dollar ring, I figured.

When you won the welterweight championship, as I did twice, the Loyal Brotherhood of Enlisted Men — which didn't exist officially, of course, but did it ever exist in reality! — awarded you a second perquisite. The kind that made your pockets jingle. I had the choice of running gambling or loan-sharking. The loan sharks got 20 per cent every two weeks. Ten or twelve thousand dollars was invested out in loans. Collection was simple — where could a deadbeat go on Corregidor? And it was all done with a social conscience — the debtor, nabbed by the military police for being in a drunken brawl, didn't have to pay interest when he was in the guard house. Still, it wasn't my thing. I gave up loan-sharking for the gambling.

The gambling was mostly blackjack and craps. I personally controlled the game for the high rollers. The little games began on pay day. They were preliminary rounds. The big game generally began two days later with the surviving winners. We didn't have a casino, but service was first class. We would tip cooks from the mess for catering and they would make up ham-and-cheese sandwiches. I let the players drink their San Miguel beer but never any hard liquor; I felt that would be unfair. After a few belts of booze, they would start making silly bets and stupid plays. The gambling concession gave me a lot of insight into people — their characters and how they dealt with risk. You could learn to read it in the eyes — even of those who thought they had poker faces.

As a private, I was making $17.85, then $30 as a PFC (Private First Class). After three to four months, the gambling concession was often paying me as much as $2,000 a month. A master sergeant told me MacArthur himself was earning only $9,000 a year. More than once, in moments of bravado, I shoved my official wages back over the desk to the paymaster, and told him to send it to the Army Relief Fund for orphans and widows.

Body Language:
Not a Beating but a Meeting

When I'm talking to someone and that person folds their arms, I know that both paths to the door of their mind have closed as well, just as a boxer will pull his arms in to repel attacks and shield vulnerabilities. It's all body language, just like the excessive ease or rigidity of a gambler betraying a bluff.

In the ring, you can tell fear, especially when your opponent has an uncontrollable change of expression that he desperately tries to hide. In that moment, hit him, and he'll fall. Sometimes you'll even miss him, and he'll fall anyway. I've done it in the ring. I've done it in the board room.

Boxing is an art. It's not about beating people to a pulp. It's doing something that will fake out the opponent so that he incorrectly sets his defence and uncertainly pursues his attack. Sound deceptive? So is chess. Body language is so often the tip-off that can secure success ... in boxing, in chess, in business or in anything else.

I had a ball. Tailor-made clothes. Unauthorised hunting trips down to Mindoro. I used to send postal money orders home to my mother, usually $200 a month. What did I need it for? The army fed and clothed me. When I came home after two years, she still had every cheque uncashed, despite the fact that this was the height of the Depression and my father's income had collapsed. She never asked me where I got it, and she never spent a cent. Nellie, Nellie where would they find your equal today?

In spring 1936, a letter arrived from the International Olympic Committee. I trembled when I got it, and it must have been an hour before I got up the courage to open it, but I was already seeing myself riding through the Brandenburg Gate in Berlin in an open-topped Mercedes, waving to the crowd with a gold medal glistening around my neck — 'Dear Mr Roach, We regret to inform you that your request to compete on behalf of the Philippines in the upcoming Olympic Games has been denied on the grounds that you are a citizen of the United States and not ...' Those, or something like them, were the words. My heart sank through the floor. First Esther's kiss-off and now this. Wasn't anyone ever going to send me some decent mail?

When now *Veteran* Al Roach, came home from the Philippines in August 1936, my reputation had preceded me. My father had been bragging that I would be the next welterweight champion of the world and was showing off the posters announcing my bouts. We went down to Stillman's gym, where Jack Dempsey and Tom Gibbons trained. All gyms smelled the same then as now: liniment and sweat.

The scene looked like the backdrop for a *cinéma noir* flick about the mob and the fight game. Staring at me was Edward G. Robinson's double in a purple shirt with a pearl tie-pin jabbed through a silk polka-dot tie, chomping on a huge Havana, and waving me inside the ropes: 'Awright, kid, get in der and show me what ya can do.'

I climbed in and spotted a flabby guy who must have tipped the scales at 185 pounds. I was only 145. In the service, we used to have a saying that a 180-pound boxer was slow as shit and twice as nasty. Shit? No way, I thought to myself, this is one big marbled piece of prime rib, ready for feasting. In my mind, I was already signing championship autographs at the exit of Madison Square Garden. Instead of working with a plan, I let my instincts take control.

Tell Your Kids:
Go Slug it Out on the Planning Field

In December 1997, I visited St Saviour's Amateur Boxing Club's gymnasium in Dublin on a Sunday morning, in a neighbourhood that reminded me of the side-streets and rough neighbourhoods I used to haunt. I watched a bunch of kids work out to a blaring boom-box. They impressed me.

The adults running the gym impressed me too with their dedication. When they asked me to speak to the kids, I said that boxing gave me the stamina, the will, the physical conditioning, and the discipline to found and run significant businesses.

After the visit, I thought about Ireland's pride, the long-legged Tony O'Reilly. Where would he be without the glory of his rugby career — the lessons he learned, the people he met, and the countless numbers he impressed with his achievements? For so many, the road to achievement begins on the playing field, a place that I call the planning field, because that's where — if you fight by instinct — you will get killed. If you plan it right, the other guy will step right into your punches — in the boxing ring and in the competitive arena of business.

Somebody whacked a bell, and I started fluttering around like a butterfly. He took my jabs, while inching around like mud in a tub. Then he murmured up close, 'Kid, you look pretty good. I won't hurt you.' Was he *ribbing me*, or what? I grinned at him and saw an opening, figuring it was time to deck this side of beef. I walloped him right in the solar plexus. He clinched for a few seconds, while he caught his breath. The next thing I knew, the ceiling unleashed a jackhammer directly at my face. A string of piston strokes — one after another — battered my jaw and flattened my nose. I disintegrated to the canvas like a collapsing hut in a Corregidor earthquake.

When I stumbled through our front door, *I* was the one who looked like a piece of meat, and my mother's first words were, 'Mother of God! Ya damned fool. You're headed for the same loony bin as your Uncle Luke....'

'No, Ma, I swear to God, I quit. If a fat, old man could do that to me, no telling what could happen with some-body in shape. *I quit!*'

The 'fat, old man' turned out to be Gus Lesnevich who won the light heavyweight NBA belt in May 1941 and the world title in the same weight class three months later! At the time, I was crestfallen. I look back today and what do I see? Being beaten to a pulp at Stillman's Gym was a door opening, not a door shutting. Fighting can be a career for only the very, very few — not for most. It can be excellent preparation for life, but not for too long. An early 'catastrophe' saved my brains from being sponge rubber today and made me settle down to some serious thinking about what I would do with my life.

Battlin' Al Roach in Corregidor as he looked in 1935/36
and as he looks today.

3

Call the Priest (1936–41)

In August 1936, Al Roach put down roots in Brooklyn, where he remained through the last months of 1937. After his ill-fated 1936 sparring encounter with future boxing champ Gus Lesnevich, Al did odd jobs, including a stint as a clerk, but steady work was scarce and he was restless. Being a New York City policeman or fireman has always been a prestigious position, and it was especially so for an Irish-American in the 1930s. The pay was good, the pension (after 20 years' service) enticing, the work steady with no lay-offs, and the role as a community servant honoured. Becoming a fireman was Al's new goal, and he took the public-service exam for a fire-department post.

While waiting for a coveted opening, Al shipped out with the Merchant Marine in January 1938. He toiled in the boiler room and as steward's mate on cargo ships carrying freight to South Africa, South America, and other exotic ports. In 1939, he returned to New York and an opening on the New York City Fire Department's Engine Company 310. The city was throbbing with World's Fair fever — that massive fair began in the spring of 1939.

Something of a daredevil and while still a Fire Department cadet, Al volunteered to participate in a series of exhibition jumps from a height of nearly fifty feet to a safety net below. A badly held net caused him to collide with the pavement on a night-time jump. He ruptured two vertebrae in his back and suffered a frightening brush with death. After many blood transfusions and a slow and painful recovery, Al resumed service with the Fire Department, but was fitted for a cumbersome back brace. Even today he suffers episodes of excruciating pain. After his return, Al's work as a hose-man was interrupted by a variety of accidents — including a serious ankle injury in 1940 and a fall off of a speeding fire engine in August 1941. US entry into the Second World War loomed on the horizon, and Al expected to be in the thick of the fray.

'Light up, and we'll have to hang you,
because it's too damn dangerous to shoot you.'

Those were the words of our rather young captain to the crew of twenty-four seamen and guards of the supply ship, assembled on her deck. We were all in fatigues and puttees. Some of the guys said Cap reminded them of what young Lucky Lindbergh looked like when he made his solo flight back in '27, except he had a seriousness on his boyish face that we all associated with Lindbergh after the baby was kidnapped in '32. Cap warned us that no smoking meant *no smoking* . .. in the head ... or on the bunk ... or anywhere else.

At first, we all thought he was joking, and all of us enlisted men chuckled. The officers didn't laugh with us. Instead, Cap grimly nodded for us to look behind where we were standing, and we saw a Manila hemp noose with thirteen coils draped over a hoist. You could see everyone's neck muscles knot up. With that, officers handed round the chewing tobacco. Countless packs of Camels, Chesterfields and Lucky Strikes were confiscated and heaved over board.

Cap then revealed the cargo we were carrying: an incredible cache of gunpowder and cartridges. Even back then I think the United States knew that conflict with Japan was inevitable, and we had to build up our stocks in strategic areas like the Philippines. A nationalist movement called the 'League of Blood' was already assassinating senior political and business leaders in Japan. When Japan invaded Manchuria in 1931, the uproar resulted in Japan leaving the League of Nations.

We and the ship were bound for the Philippines and travelled at a crawl, no faster than 8–10 knots. To this day, I don't know how they cooked on board. It was 1933, and my first true sea voyage. I mention it now because it really is also the beginning of a new era for me, the fourteen-year period from 1933 to 1947, when staying out of the reaches of fire played a pivotal role in my life. For a person with a natural fire in their belly, tempting fire immediately around you can be an incinerating experience.

When I came back from being in the army in Corregidor, I took the civil-service exam. Rather than sitting around waiting for the results, I shipped out with the US Merchant Marine. Although no one tattooed Jean Harlow on my chest, and I didn't smoke opium or pot in the seething dens of Panama, the Merchant Marine showed me a rough-and-tumble side of life that my army days only hinted at.

On one voyage through the Canal in the Merchant Marine, we had leave in Panama City, not a common stop for us. The Captain wanted to keep a close rein on the crew, I suspect, because he didn't know the port well. On the night before we berthed, he addressed the crew in a very matter-of-fact way. In truth, you could barely hear him, which is the right volume to talk at when you want somebody to listen to you. His speech was along the following lines: 'I know you guys know all about gonorrhoea and syphilis. And I'm not going to bore you with any moral lectures. But I think you should be aware that in Panama City they have just had a rather serious outbreak of a disease called the tropical *jallilies*. Public health authorities say it can be contracted from some of the young ladies in the horizontal profession.

'If you're infected, you'll think nothing happened right afterwards. However, on about the tenth day after having been exposed, be very careful about shaking it when you take a leak. If you do, and if you are *jallilies* positive, it may plop off right into the urinal. I've seen it happen, and it's not a pretty sight.' The captain paused briefly and smiled brightly. 'Well, I just wanted to mention that,' he went on. 'Men, you've done a great job on this voyage, and I hope that you all have the rest and relaxation you deserve on shore leave. Good night.'

Nobody went near the girls, not even for a dance. We kept running into each other sightseeing in little *carretas*. We heard rumours some of the guys might even have gone to a missionary church on land.

During the Second World War, I asked an epidemiologist from a New York Hospital just how serious the *jallilies* epidemic was in Panama during the 1930s and he nearly choked on the olive in his martini, he was laughing so hard.

Before long, I found myself being asked to help organise a seaworkers' union and to walk the picket line with the seaworkers. I was persuaded by the guys to run as union steward in an election on the docks. Being pretty new on the job, I wondered how all this was going to happen. My buddies said, '*No problem*, the election is wired.'

'*Wired?*' I didn't like the sound of this.

'That's the way it's done here. First we get a union. Then we get tough, smart people into the key jobs. *Then* we'll have democracy.'

'OK, whatever you say.'

It was just before the morning break. A guy came walking towards us, brushing his palms together and beaming.

'All set,' he said. He had just stuffed and sealed the ballot box. 'You just won the election five-to-one, Roach. Let's go to breakfast.' The four of us piled over to the diner across the street for hash browns and scrambled eggs.

We came back, and I looked up at the blackboard hung on a pillar. There I saw the results posted in chalk on the slate: I had *lost* the election 148 to 3. We didn't even get the four votes that would have come from me and the three guys who took me to breakfast! When he learned about it, a union old-timer shook his head at me and said, 'Roach, you dope, never go to breakfast in the middle of a union election.'

The opposition had just switched the ballot box stuffed for their guy with the one that had been stuffed for me.

A Political Primer

- No one can ever guarantee you will win a secret ballot, because if it's truly secret, it isn't fixed.

- No one can ever guarantee you will win a fixed election, unless you're backed up by power down a gun barrel, in which case you don't need an election anyway.

- People who go around trying to fix elections or contests or shows of sympathy are generally as short-sighted as they are dishonest and are bound to screw up the details somewhere.

- Almost everything you win that's fixed costs more time and energy to fix than to win honestly, and that's not counting the extortion people end up paying to blackmailers to cover up the fact that they fixed something in the first place.

- The hardest thing in the world to control is a secret. If you tell two people a secret, you have just told twenty more, because each of them will tell ten others. Remember, the *law of secrets*: $1 + 1 \neq 2$. $1 + 1 = 11$.

The steward on one Merchant Marine ship was a great old guy with a walrus moustache and a limp like Walter Brennan in *To Have and Have Not*. Stew was from Hamburg. One day, he was feeling poorly and asked me to replenish the ship's wares in the port of Durban, South Africa. He told me not to trust anyone at the ship's chandler and to count all the goods and money twice. Then Stew gave me a considerable wad of cash, totalling $650. I got the supplies, double-checked everything, and paid the bill of $620.

When I returned to ship, I handed Stew his $30 in change and was walking out of his cabin when he spat out through his moustache, 'Roach, wait just one minute. Where's my sixty dollars?' Stew meant the personal cash rebate of 10 per cent from the Arab owner of that supplier for bringing the ship's business to that store. The supplier had actually handed me the kickback and said, 'That's for you.' I naïvely thought he meant *me* and not the person I was working for. I said 'Thank you very much', and pocketed it. Ultimately I got $6.20 — 1 per cent of the deal, not 10 per cent — and learned from the experience that the crudest of kickbacks and the most honest of commissions and gratuities are rarely purely personal rewards. They have a system to them like anything else in business.

In 1939, I traded in my sailor's scarf for a fireman's helmet. Being a fireman never goes out of your blood, even when you've been retired for half a century. All over the world, I still like to drop in on fire stations. I've done it in Paris, in New York, everywhere. Next trip to China, I'm going to do it in Beijing. I never knew why seaman were actually preferred as fire-fighters nor had I ever understood why fire-fighting ranks followed the precedent of naval ranks, until I met up with District Officer Tom Geraghty of the venerable Tara Street Station in Dublin. Tommy is something of a scholar on the history of fire-fighting. In a nutshell, here's what he explained were the four key reasons why naval men were preferred for the newly emerging fire-fighting departments of the nineteenth century:

- Naval people were used to working together in small groups and at close quarters, as they did on ship.

- They were 'experts in rigging' and ropes so they could handle heights and tackle.

- They dealt in 'canvas', which equipped them to master the early safety nets.

- They were 'disciplined' decision-makers because of the 'law of the sea' that required quick calls in often complex situations.

Yes, Marina
There is an Adam Smith

Marina Dorokhova is an extremely competent administrator for our ABS biotechnology firm in Russia. It would be hard to imagine a more honest and conscientious person, or a more perceptive one. On a visit to Moscow several years ago, not long after the beginning of the turn away from Communism, I asked Marina to take me and several associates to a store where we could purchase some quality Russian art.

Without hesitation, she found us the best spot in town. She translated, helped us select, and completed the transaction. She gave me the change down to the last rouble. As we were leaving, the owner stuck a wad of bills in Marina's hand. Immediately, she handed it to me and said, 'Mr Roach, I'm sorry, I underestimated your change.'

'No, no, Marina, that's your commission for bringing the business to this store. It's a legitimate commission. Enjoy it.'

'Mr Roach, is this what Adam Smith meant by a market economy?'

'Well, Marina, yes, I think it is.'

With a warm smile lighting up her intelligent face, and after — I'm sure — a quick comparison with the sorry earnings she had endured in the Communist era, she turned to me and said, 'Mr Roach, I think I'm going to *like* capitalism!'

I wanted a job where I could help save lives, and it was certain that I wasn't going to be a doctor, as I had sometimes dreamed in my youth. It wasn't until nearly fifty years after I had served in the Merchant Marine that I learned what a natural transition it was from my life at sea to my next career.

The Fire Department accepted me. In an Irish-American family of the 1930s, if you attained the coveted access to the cops or the Fire Department, you had made it. The instructor, Chief Ryan, told us, 'All of a sudden, all you people are going to look very *beau-ti-ful*, very pretty.'

Ryan was six-four, a bruiser of an army sergeant from the First World War. 'Clark Gable can't compare. All the mothers will hover around you. Then the girls will, too. It isn't the uniforms. It's not the blue that makes you beautiful, lads. It's the pension. The mothers know you get a lifetime pension in twenty years. Even should you die, God forbid, the wife gets a huge salary award.'

My new identity: Firehat number 9957 serving Engine Company 310 at the intersection of Nostrand and Snyder. This was in the heart of the Williamsburg and Brownsville neighbourhoods and full of fire hazards. If you got high marks in probationary school, that's where you got assigned. My mother must have added ten inches to her height on hearing the news. And true to Ryan's prophecy, the robustly built Patricia happened to bump into me on my way to work ... and the blushing Rosalie gave me her place in line at the bus stop. This one came on, and that one came on harder. Daughters that we never knew people had streamed out of the woodwork like fillies out of the starting gate at the Empire City racetrack.

During fire school, I was the class daredevil. Gus Lesnevich might have extinguished my ring aspirations, but he hadn't cooled my spirit a single degree. One particular exercise gave almost everybody shivers down their spine. Not me, I loved it. It was to climb a four-storey building with a scaling ladder. Then you turned around at about the third storey and jumped into a safety net. A lot of guys didn't want to do that, but I would swan-dive down, spin in flight, and land on my butt to the surprise and anger of the trainers. The exercise also helped the other trainees learn how to catch people in a net. For me, it was just like a circus acrobat hurtling into a trampoline.

At about the same time I joined the Fire Department, the New York World's Fair opened. The Fair electrified the city in 1939–40, and I went to visit it in May 1939, just after it opened and before I began Fire Department training. With the Fair, New Yorkers thought we had truly arrived. We had a skyline — the Chrysler Building and the Empire State Building were each less than ten years old. So many visitors thronging to New York and to the Fair! So many sights! One exhibit astonished my twenty-three-year-old eyes. It was at the RCA pavilion. It didn't look fancy. Still, I had a funny inkling that it would someday revolutionise the world as a teaching tool that would cross national boundaries. It was the first public unveiling of the television set in America. Many thought it was the first public exhibition of television anywhere. But regular television shows were already being broadcast from an experimental station in the United States as early as 1931. The technology and the time — the Fair was billed as the World of Tomorrow — all seemed so exciting.

Having been in the Fire Department for one month, and while still in the probationary period, Chief Ryan stopped me in the hall and said, 'Roach, I got a grand, grand job for you. It'll go on your record. You're gonna be famous. It's the old safety net jump from training school, but the ladders are a little higher. You'll be up about fifty feet.' In case I was in any doubt, he continued, 'Lad, you're going to be the star of the New York World's Fair. His Honour Mayor LaGuardia, the Little Flower himself, will be there to admire you and applaud you.'

What could I say? First, MacArthur pats me on the back. Then LaGuardia. I was going to be right up there with Sergeant Alvin York and Charles Lindbergh on the roster of America's men of daring. Maybe, just maybe they would even beam pictures of Al Roach on that RCA television gadget to some far-off place.

So, with my consent, Ryan volunteered me for this exhibition as part of the Fire Prevention Week festivities.

Twenty-three times I appeared at the World's Fair Grounds in Flushing Meadows. Twenty-three times I ascended into the autumn afternoon sky surrounding New York City. Sometimes it was bright blue and warm, sometimes it was nippy and steely grey. A ladder was perched across two erect aerial ladders, and the jumper had to walk to the centre of it. I didn't mind the jumping, but walking on that ladder sometimes bothered me. Still, every jump I made landed directly in the centre of the net like a dart sailing into a bullseye.

'Hey, Cap, where's the Mayor? Haven't seen him yet.'

'Oh, he'll be there tonight, son. Want to jump tonight, do you?'

'Sure, I do. You say the Mayor will be there. Then, I'm jumping for sure.'

10 October 1939. Jump twenty-four. It's night-time and I scale upward and tread carefully to the centre of the cross ladder. No problem. I've done this, too, in training and mounted heights as great at sea. Ready? Someone yells from the ground. *'Ready!'* shouts the next Errol Flynn, wearing Badge 9957 and poised to become the pride of New York.

Suddenly the beams of two 2,000-candlepower floodlights flip on, aimed directly at my head, as someone shouts out *'JUMP!'*

'Jump where?' I yell back. *'I can't see a thing!'*

'Just jump and we'll catch you.'

OK, Chief, I think to myself, anything for you ... and

the Department ... and the Mayor; and down I sail.

It seems like hours later, and the same bright lights are glaring at me.

'I thought I jumped.'

'You did.'

'Where am I?'

'Flushing Hospital.'

My eyes waver in and out of focus. Finally I realise I'm on my back and the lights blazing in my eyes are the ceiling lamps of the operating theatre.

I had jumped 47 feet. To this day, I don't know exactly what happened. Maybe the ground team was swaying around trying to get me just perfect. Probably they were holding the net too slack. I landed in it, but the net and I both hit the pavement below with a nasty crunch. They said I muttered one sentence: 'Don't tell Mom, call priest.' Then I was out cold. It took artificial respiration to start my heart again. They rushed me to the hospital. I suffered concussion and ruptured the fourth and fifth lumbar vertebrae. The transfusions were numerous. I wavered in and out of consciousness.

What do you fear most after an accident like that? Recently I read the autobiography of the heroic American actor Christopher Reeve, whose fall while horseback riding was far worse than my accident. Nonetheless, my thought processes were similar, especially that horrible recognition right after you survive a terrible accident but fear that you will be permanently disabled. Reeve writes,

> ...it had dawned on me that I was going to be a huge burden to everybody, that I had ruined my life and everybody else's.*

Ultimately, I recovered, but it required great perseverance to do so, and it would never have happened without the powerful encouragement of fellow firemen who would

---

* Reeve, Christopher. *Still Me*. New York: Random House, 1998, p. 32.

take their personal time to transport me to and from therapy sessions at hospitals and at the YMCA. Psychologically, President Franklin Roosevelt was a tremendous inspiration too, especially photos I saw of him swimming in the heated pools at Warm Springs, Georgia. But my admiration didn't stop there. I was in awe of his recovery from the polio with which he had been stricken in 1921, his determination to go on to fight for the presidency, his personal chartering of a Ford Tri-Motor to fly him to the 1932 Democratic Convention where he could explain the New Deal to the delegates and win the nomination, and his gutsy handling of the problems of the Depression.

My accident happened shortly after my probation period. In fact, almost all of my front-line fire-fighting experience occurred *after* the accident. That experience came to me in batches, because I was intermittently on light and on regular duty. Slowly, I began to learn the dreaded periods of a fireman's life. Christmas, for example, is one of the happiest times of the year for me, but, to this day, I wouldn't have a natural Christmas tree in my home. I can remember two awful fires caused by candles on natural trees. In one of them, little children died.

Throughout my life, I've always had the good fortune to have other people take an interest in me and help me learn the ropes when I tried something new. So it was at the Fire Department. After my abrupt fall, I was on and off the trucks, depending on whether my legs held or gave way. A Jewish guy — I believe his name was Benny Rubin — was the hose-man for our company and he broke me in as a back-up hose-man.

Pound-for-pound, he had more survival wisdom than nearly anybody I've ever met. 'Don't run in to the goddamn basement, until you judge how sturdy the main floor is.' 'Don't get too close to that heavy player piano, because it can go through the floor, and you'll go right along with it.' 'Don't be caught in the backdraft.' After I got seared once, Benny taught me to wear the thickest sweaters and wool coats underneath the waterproof fire jackets. This wasn't to fight the cold, although it was always harder to fight a fire in the depth of winter; it was the only way to protect against the surge of heat that could char your skin. Most of all, Benny understood the survival power of the nozzle *for the fireman*. Smoke was a lot tougher then, because the personal safety gear was so much more primitive. But the hose-man had a constant source of oxygen. He would put his nose near that water jet and the ventilation of the water mist would flush his face and his lungs. Benny's suggestion of becoming a protégé hose-man was invaluable.

The hose-man was like the surgeon in the fire fight. He was the number-one weapon. He carried only the nozzle. Everyone else pulled the weight. Every good team learned 'Don't exhaust the hose-man.' A fire will flare in different spots. He zaps it here, and he zaps it there. The fires I remember most vividly were the small single-family home or duplex blazes. There you could mean the difference to survival of just one family. The multiple-alarm blazes were like huge military campaigns, and you felt like you were just an ant scurrying among the multitude.

When you fight fires or do anything in life, it's vital to show up in the right place. A few years back, I remember a guy who was half-jugged going into the wrong side of a two-screen theatre in Dublin showing *Jaws* on one screen and *Towering Inferno* on the other. He passed out and woke up half way into the *Inferno*. After twenty minutes of firestorms and collapsing ceilings, he yelled out: 'All well and good, but where's the feckin' fish?'

**Fire-fighting is Fire-fighting
Be the Blaze in Business or in Buildings**

I have extinguished real fires and figurative ones for half a century. The principles for fighting fires in both is more alike than different. Here's a checklist:

How good's your early warning system? Old firehouses, even in the middle of cities, had large towers from which sentinels could spot telltale smoke. Are your people and your information systems standing guard duty over the assets of your business? Do they have a clear and unobstructed view of what's going on?

How quickly can you respond to an emergency? A good engine company is out the door in forty seconds or less. When your business last had a problem, how long did it fester before people dug in and started to solve it?

How good is your communication? Contact in a fire station used to be hollering into tubes on brass switchboards. Today, businesses have cell-phones and e-mail, and yet the most natural tendency — and the most dangerous one — is to stop communicating during a crisis. From day one in the Fire Department, they hammered into our heads that the foremost task of the first unit on the scene is to size up whether further units will be needed. Get ample resources to the blaze early! Are your troubleshooters conditioned to think the same way?

Are you training people to measure risks? As Benny Rubin would put it, 'Is the piano going through the floor or not?' Tailor your response to the situation at hand. Not all problems can be solved the same way, and even the lightest tactic in an already overloaded situation can cause everything to cave in under you.

We all got paid the same, but the hook-and-ladder men got more medals, because they were doing things in the middle of the blaze — opening up the ventilation and pulling the victims free. Usually the hose-man was first into the fire, but he could never get the medal, because he couldn't let go of that goddamn hose to do something spectacular that the papers would give prominence to. There was a constant professional rivalry between the hose team and the hook-and-ladder guys. After a fire, we would always be ready for a big meal, whereas they would be nauseous and couldn't have kept a thing down.

From the ceremony and recognition side, being a fireman was a source of great pride to me. Like most of the Fire Department force, I marched in the big St Patrick's Day parade down Fifth Avenue in Manhattan. We did it in full uniform and on our own time. Every Italian holiday, the sky was blue. Every Jewish holiday, the sun glowed. Every Spanish holiday, it was *buen tiempo*. But each March the St Patrick's Day parade was marred by sleet and slush. I thought we Irish must be on the wrong side!

I would ride on the back of the hose engine and generally managed to stay on board. In August 1941, we were crossing Church Avenue in Flatbush, returning from a fire and going pretty fast. Suddenly I was thrown off of the engine. The ambulance raced me to Bellevue Hospital where doctors diagnosed a serious ligamentary sprain. That put me off active duty for two months. Increasingly I was on watch duty and assigned to the firehouse. Inevitably, I was concerned about where this would lead, and whether I'd be able to last out the twenty years' service needed for the pension.

My personal trials as a fireman seemed considerable, but all of us would soon be dwarfed by drama and suffering on an unimaginable scale. In 1941, a new era of firefighting was ushered into American history, and it began on a Sunday morning in December. West Virginia, California, Nevada and Arizona were the sites. Not the states, but the smouldering decks of these namesake warships after Japanese air power made its devastating strike at Pearl Harbor. I was mad as hell. While I couldn't hang onto a fire truck too well, and I didn't much take to warfare, I was determined to enlist the lethal weapons of my two fists and whatever more was in me on Uncle Sam's behalf.

4

On the Waterfront (1941–52)

In December 1941, just after Pearl Harbor, Al Roach volunteered for service in the US Navy, with hopes of an assignment in London, where he heard the British were commissioning New York firemen as officers to help combat blazes resulting from German air attacks. He was almost accepted, until screening physicians discovered his back brace and rejected him for service. Dejected, he returned to his fire department post, but his prospects there were increasingly dim. A back sprain in November 1941 put Al on the light-duty roster. From 1941 until War's end, he was a supervisor and instructor of a bomb squad patrolling the New York docks and protecting them from enemy saboteurs.

During 1943–47, several important personal events occurred. In January 1943, Al married Dorothy Menke in Brooklyn, and between 1943 and 1947 all three of their children were born. During the War, Al's two-year-old niece Patsy was hospitalised with a severe streptococcal infection. Unable to secure the smallest dose of penicillin, Patsy died in the arms of her uncle Al, the hospital fire warden at the time. In 1946, Al's parents' home was destroyed by fire, and he underwent a serious back operation in 1945.

In 1947, not long after the family fire, Al was discharged from the fire department. With a wife and soon three children and without a high-school diploma, his future seemed uncertain. He was better off than most, receiving a disability pension of $193.87 per month but felt it was unfair to go back to school full-time. Instead, in 1948 he took a light labour job on the New York docks as a checker. Then in June 1952 a second trauma — a protruding stake on an open-bed truck slammed him from behind, fractured his neck, ended his new career, and made him an invalid once more.

'Who or What the Hell is A Roach, ROACH?'

A bunch of guys — I'm one of them — milling around a navy examination station in our skivvies, waiting to have tongue depressors jabbed into our throats, and worse things done to our rear ends. Given the dismal state we're all in, everybody sniggers at the question about The Roach.

I finally figure they might be talking about me. 'Here, Sir.' I raise my hand. 'This is A. Roach. Check me out, and you'll see I'm a *He* not a *What*.'

The guys all chuckle, and I know I'm going to pay for the wisecrack. A skinny middle-aged doctor with horn-rimmed glasses storms towards me, wearing a huge reflecting disk on a band around his head, with his open lab coat flowing behind him. I feel sure this guy laughed at his last joke in 1924 when Will Rogers said, 'Everything is funny as long as it is happening to somebody else.'

'Roach,' he asks impatiently, 'is this *your* brace?'

'It is,' I answer.

He frowns. 'How in the world do you think you can qualify for military service if you have to wear a gizmo like this?'

'It's not that big a deal. I'm a hose-man with the New York Fire Department.'

'You drag a heavy firehose during the day and wear a night-brace like that after hours. Are you out of your mind? Do you want to end up in a wheelchair for life?'

I don't answer and he continues, 'You're the first guy I've run into in three weeks who wanted to slip his way *into* Service as opposed to trying to worm his way out of it. Your ideals may be noble, but you're still wasting my time. Get dressed and get out of here.'

On the way out of the induction station, I walk down the barren December sidewalk and kick an empty sardine can with all of my might.

The bombing of Britain during the fall of 1940 outraged

me. During the Battle of Britain, I read in the papers of the fifty-seven consecutive nights of bombings, and that firemen in London who tried to leave the fire department to join the British Army were considered cowards, trying to get out of the crosshairs of the Junker bomb sights. When I saw that, I figured that here was a chance for a fireman to fulfil his ultimate destiny. After all, plenty of Irish were in England too, making a good bob or two working in the arms factories, if not serving in the ranks of the British military. Guys at the station said the British were recruiting some former civilian firemen from the US Navy and commissioning some of them as lieutenant commanders — they thought veterans of the New York Fire Department had the best credentials. I figured 'What the hell?' — volunteered for the navy — passed the first physical — still breathing? — made it — figured that no one would ever notice the brace in the pile of clothes on the side of the room. But I didn't clear the hurdle of the final physical.

During the War, I was confined to New York, to the fire department, and mostly to light duty. To my liking, the duty was sometimes dangerous. In 1941, I received a diploma for Incendiary, Explosive and War Gas Control from the Fire Department Fire College. The major theatre for sabotage risk was vital shipping out of New York. Slowly I was being drawn back to the docks so memorable in my youth for my father's career.

I encountered my share of suspicious packages wrapped in plain, brown paper. Did we defuse any bombs? Well, I can say no instances were ever reported in the papers. Fortunately, sabotage never amounted to much during the Second World War, probably because the vigilance — after Pearl Harbor — was so great. In fact, the only actual attempt at sabotage was perpetrated by two gangs of saboteurs landing on Long Island and on the Florida coast respectively. Both actions were thwarted, and, by early August 1942, six of the eight arrested had been executed in Washington. *The Normandie* — a ship of French origin taken over for conversion into a troop carrier — was accidentally set on fire in New York harbour, although many initially thought it was sabotage.

When I think of the War, I remember one little package I held that made me tremble more than any bomb I was asked to disarm — indeed, more than any I have held before or since. In fact, the memory makes me weep without restraint even today. She was just two years old, and her name was Patsy Lynch.

Remember those babies, with the adorable smile and irresistible lick of hair on top of their heads that adorn babyfood jars? Patsy Lynch, born just about a year after Pearl Harbor, could have been the model for one of them. She was my sister Annie's baby — Annie, my ward; Annie with the auburn hair, that glistened in the sunlight, who, when asked by the neighbours how one could get such a lustrous mane, would answer with a smile, 'Choose your parents well!' Patsy was just like her mother.

Part of my duty assignment was to serve as fire warden and watch officer in New York's King's County Hospital. I was a regular to many doctors and nurses. When Annie's little daughter Patsy took sick, I'm not ashamed to say that I used every bit of clout I could muster to get her into the best paediatric wing I could. The doctors did a culture. It was a streptococcal throat infection.

Day after day, when my night watch shifts were over, I would go to Patsy's ward. The agony the toddler was in seemed unbearable. There was abdominal pain and nausea. Then her face developed a bright flush. It could well have been scarlatina, a by-product of the streptococcal infection. The crying was incessant, but it was weak — not a healthy childhood illness, but something insidious. I remember vividly the soft crying and the hollow echoing steps of my boots down the long linoleum hallway, with the occasional swinging of a fire-door as a nurse rushed by, shaking a thermometer or carrying a steel pan with a sponge.

The diagnosis of the doctors was unanimous. Patsy needed just one thing — an injection of penicillin. Just one injection, they felt, would ensure her recovery. Without it, her chances grew slimmer with each day. Even in the drug's relatively short lifespan, it had saved countless children who had fallen victim to streptococcal throat infections and scarlet fever. There was only one problem: this was war time, and penicillin was rationed. Fleming hadn't discovered the effects of penicillin until 1928 and wasn't even knighted for it until 1944. War conditions put penicillin into the hands of a few key policy-makers.

The supply of penicillin in New York was controlled by medical authorities, headquartered in Boston. Countless pleas came from New York to make a dose of penicillin available for an innocent two-year-old — the same dosage that would have been needed to cure a reckless GI of a bout of venereal disease, contracted after some drunken binge in the back alleys of New Orleans or Tiajuana. Boston was unyielding.

One afternoon, Patsy and I were walking up and down the hallway. An adult holding her was the only thing that seemed to provide any comfort. We walked and waited for any news from Boston. Her breathing became shallower. Then it just stopped. She was gone. The doctors had warned me it would happen just that way.

My sister Margaret came back by train from her convent mission in Lowell, Massachusetts, for the funeral. In the tiny casket, Patsy looked like a doll. Jay, the undertaker, had put a bonnet on her because of the deep laceration made in her forehead as part of the treatment the doctors had attempted to keep her alive. For the funeral, they were going to put the little white casket in the trunk of a car instead of in a large hearse. The thought made Annie hysterical. Margaret suggested instead that Annie sit in the front of the car, and Margaret would carry the casket on her lap.

The image and the experience never left me: a tiny casket on the lap of a nun, sitting on the back seat of a car, needlessly headed to a cemetery, owing to intransigent policy, driven by a war (no matter how defensible), that had ignited thousands of miles away because men couldn't reason with one another. Had we grown more civilised or merely more formal and better organised in our brutality and in our abuse of the most basic human goals?

How Can You Tell if a
War-time Decision is Humane?

- Does it support the long-term needs of the society?
- Does it advocate the interests of children and their mothers?
- Is it consistent with the goals that even men at war espouse?
- Does it apply the best of our technology to advance the ends of those at dire risk, who nonetheless have a clear chance to live a productive life?
- Is it unilateral and unbending, or does some mechanism exist for appeal under special circumstances?

Part of the therapy that went into my recovery from the World's Fair accident was physical training. That meant working out at home and often outside, without a shirt and in a pair of swimming trunks. The fighter's build had stayed with me and apparently interested at least one young lady in the neighbourhood, although I didn't know it at the time. Her name was Dorothy Menke, an unusually attractive blonde, several years younger than myself. While we took to each other, I was considered kind of a worldly guy, and her father — a strict German Lutheran — was adamantly against the marriage. He was also convinced I would be a cripple for life, after the big accident.

Cupid prevailed over caution. We were married on 9 January 1943 in St Brendan's Church, by the priest who had overseen Dorothy's conversion to Catholicism. On the first night of our honeymoon in the Catskills, I started to fill the tub to take a nice hot bath. Diverted by what was happening in the bedroom, I forgot about what was underway in the bath. As I drew back the sheets on the bed, I suddenly realised that I was stepping into water. The edges of the sheets were drenched. The water was sloshing down from the bathroom into the bedroom.

The next instant, fists thundered against our door. Red in the face, I answered and this guy was staring me down with a furious look on his face. 'Are you by chance on your honeymoon?' he asked.

I nodded and offered to pay for any damage. He walked away, shaking his head, but I could see a smile at the corner of his mouth.

'Forget it,' he said knowingly. 'I'll have the bellboy come up and move you to a different room.'

After the move was over, Dorothy, who had been totally disconcerted by the event, was nearly in a daze. Eyeing me in my shorts, she took stock of my 5 foot 9½ inch frame, which she had often seen outdoors, working out with Indian clubs. Having paused thoughtfully, she pronounced, 'You know, Al, if your legs were longer, you'd be much taller.'

This is going to be one interesting marriage, I thought to myself, and I haven't been disappointed.

My wife loves animals, especially her herd of almost 150 Nubian goats on her farm in Puerto Rico. She had been away from the mainland for an extended time, overseeing construction of a cathouse — more exactly, a house for cats, nine of them, and they seem to have more fun with the toys and gadgets in it than I used to have at Coney Island. I decided to surprise her with some renovations in our home in New York. On the ground floor, where the master bedroom had been, I installed an advanced new whirlpool, large enough that you could swim against an artificially induced current. My wife walked through the door of our home. Before I could announce the interior design changes, she breezed into what she thought was still the bedroom, flinging her luxurious designer coat onto a bubbling tank of heated water, where the bed had once been.

Moral: If you have a bedroom secret to share, do it early.

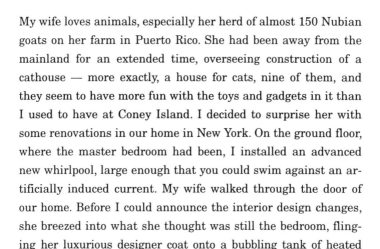

I don't mean to give the impression that the War was removed from our daily lives. Two of my brothers were overseas in the conflict — Joey in the navy, and Jimmy in the army. Both had volunteered. My brother Eddie had five kids and was exempted; Herbie was too young.

We lived in daily dread of a telegram informing us that something had happened to Joey or Jimmy. In the summer of 1945, my sister Margaret woke up screaming, 'I know he needs me.' She was convinced that Jimmy was in grave danger. Her screams awakened the other nuns and Sister Superior suggested they all say a rosary, which they did. Almost immediately afterwards, we learned that Jimmy was on Okinawa. The Japanese had asked for peace, but then launched a sneak attack on 15 August 1945. The Japanese closed in and shelled the crowded foxholes. The guys in the foxholes perished. The ones who were still out in the open — Jimmy included — survived. Both Jimmy and Joey made it back alive.

There were threats abroad and threats at home. The fire I missed was, predictably, the one that struck my own family. It happened in June 1946. While the fire took place in Brooklyn, an eerie smoke alarm was triggered in Margaret's Dominican convent in Lowell, Massachusetts. In the middle of the night, Margaret again woke up screaming. 'It's my father, it's my father' she insisted, though hundreds of miles away. 'Something's happened.'

Once more, Sister Superior decided the nuns should say a rosary in the chapel, and they did. The phone rang at six in the morning with news from Brooklyn and she learned that our father had had a small stroke. Later she found out that it was the result of a terrible fire caused by a short-circuit. Thus the second of two vivid and remarkable premonitions in Margaret's life.

My parents had recently made the last mortgage payment on the home they had moved into twenty-three years earlier and worked so hard to own. They had just had it painted and had some electrical work done.

On this particular evening, Herbie had walked our mother down to visit our sister Helen. He and his friend Leo then went to the movies. Meanwhile my father had left home earlier with Jimmy and Joey. They wanted to see Joe Louis defend his title, and a local beer garden was the only place around that had a TV.

Then the bells and sirens of the fire engines filled the neighbourhood. Somebody yelled into the tavern that the Roach house was burning. Dad, Jimmy, and Joey all tried to get into the house, believing that our mother was still there. The fire-fighters found my father but had to carry him out because he was overcome with smoke. Jimmy was singed. Herbie, who had left the movie early, appeared on the scene, and tried to explain to Jimmy that our mother wasn't inside — she was at Helen's.

My parents rebuilt the home, but it took eight months, and almost all of their personal possessions had been lost, as were many of my travel souvenirs.

And where was I while all this was going on? At Yankee Stadium, watching Joe Louis knock out Billy Conn in the eighth round. I was not on duty that night, and soon my fire-fighting duty would end altogether. When I was told I would be retired from the fire department, in the year after my parents' fire, it was psychologically devastating. I worried that my family would think, 'My God, he lost a good job. What's going to happen to him? He'll be little better than an invalid for the rest of his life.'

When I got my first fireman's pension cheque it was $193.87. The doctor who discharged me had said, 'Buddy, you can live pretty good on that because it's tax-free. The average monkey is out there bringing home $30–40 a week. You got close to fifty bucks a week net. That's one hell of a base.' (Now that cheque is up to $2,400 a month because of cost-of-living adjustments.)

With three kids (by 1947, AP, Dorothy and Tim had all arrived), I didn't think it would be right to go to college full time. I was still struggling with my own identity, unsure whether I was a blue-collar guy or had the potential to do more. Once again, the door was shutting, and I was having the damnedest time figuring out which new door to open.

In any case, I thought it would be wise to hold down some sort of paying work. So I found a job as a checker on the docks. What does a checker do? He verifies that the merchandise listed on the shipping manifest has actually been delivered, in good condition and in the quantity specified. Elia Kazan's 1954 movie *On the Waterfront* — with Marlon Brando, Rod Steiger and Karl Malden — is a riveting and accurate account of life on the New York docks at that time. It was a brutal and unforgiving school of hard knocks.

Make Your Pension Your Launching Pad

I've been getting a pension of one sort or another for more than half a century. At first I thought that I might retire; then I realised I never would. Folks are living longer and fuller lives. More and more people will be receiving pensions while they are still active. Use your pension as a survival crutch, and I guarantee you that is what you will do — eke out your survival until they bury or burn the remains.

- *Plan for your pension.* That does not mean plan on how you will live *on* your pension, but how you will use your pension to give you basic economic security. And then start thinking about the exciting stuff.

- *Make your pension the rocket fuel for your dreams.* What have you always wanted to do that working and raising a family prevented you from doing?

- *Pensions should fund tuition.* Go back to school! If you want to live a long time, you're going to need fresh skills to stay alive. Learn about computers or negotiation or public speaking. Make sure your spouse does, too.

I saw the docks when the corruption was at its heyday and before the reform efforts began. I saw whole truckloads of stuff disappear. 'But, I just checked that entire load...' I would protest.

'Hey, mind your own business,' the guy with the loud striped tie would say, patting the vest pocket of his sharkskin suit, and you knew the bulge he was thumping wasn't his bifocal case. Then there were the fights — with grappling hooks, crowbars, and marlinspikes (spikes about 6 inches long used for separating rope strands when they are being spliced). I remember one guy in an Eisenhower jacket biting off a thug's ear and spitting it out like a watermelon seed. Sometimes the cops would appear after the free-for-alls and ask you if you would like to make a statement. You'd look at the cop as if he just dropped all his marbles or you'd ask him if he could recommend a funeral parlour with a good rate for talkative dock workers.

My family had known Teddy Gleason — the famous waterfront union organiser and president of the International Longshoremen's Association union for nearly a quarter of a century — since he was a child. He was one of *us* — from our neighbourhood. When I left the fire department, it was only natural that I 'network' back to people from the neighbourhood who had made it. Teddy was a dapper Irishman, very talkative and personable, always fashionably dressed, and constantly sporting a Fedora hat. Teddy and my father both helped me to get a job as a checker on the docks.

The checkers did the verification. The head checker's job was a powerful one — to supervise the checkers and to fill out the paper work that went with the shipment. Just working for hourly wages was all right, but the head checker also participated in a lucrative gratuity system.

On my first day, the chief checker gave me a lecture along these lines (I've deleted the expletives, but every fourth word begins with the letter 'f' and ends with the letter 'g'): 'Let's say a guy has a very small load and he wants to jump the line and have his goods checked in now rather than waiting four hours. It's up to the head checker to ask the right question. The right question always is: "How much is it worth to you to advance your spot in line?"' Remember, the line is always the line, and its order is cast in concrete, *except* when the head checker determines it is in the best interest of the line to be different [that is, when some guy with a small load shoves a wad of bills into the head checker's pocket to make an exception.]

Not every head checker was like that, but there were many more like that in those days than there are today.

The small load would be dispatched over to the side of the dock, and a couple of extra dockworkers would re-pack it onto hand-trucks. The head checker *always* had permission to advance a small batch on hand-trucks.

Did that wad of dollars stay in the head-checker's pocket? By no means. Just like the chandler's kickback in the Merchant Marine, everybody got a piece of the buy — except that most of the pieces went to the bosses on the docks and not to the workers.

Tricks were played on all sides. 'Cradling the crates' was the favoured way to short a load so that the dockworkers could steal merchandise from the floor. Imagine a square pallet is stacked with boxes five high and three across. That makes forty-five boxes. *Except*, if the centre stack is empty. Then there are only forty boxes in the shipment. And the thieves are five the richer. By mid-afternoon, the checkers are often too weary to stand on their tip-toes and peer into the centre of the pallet. It's a perfect set-up. Sometimes, the experienced cradler will go a step further and fill the central hole with empty boxes. That kind of theft is exceedingly hard to crack.

In life, it is wise to check EVERYTHING, especially what you can't see and what you assume to be there, even if you have to stand on your tiptoes to do it.

My dock experiences made me reconsider completely my position on organised labour. After a passing flirtation with workers' rights as a youngster, my view on unions had been indifferent to negative. When I was still in grade school, I ended up in a march on Fourteenth Street in Manhattan because our civics teacher said we should go there and watch people march for rights granted by the Constitution. He said that they were being falsely accused as Communists just because they were protesting. My father nearly killed me when I told him. 'You're mingling with these goddamn Communists,' he raged.

My father took a stiff view of opponents of free enterprise. He bitterly opposed the dole, which he thought could easily become a pernicious addiction. The strength of his hostility guaranteed that I never collected a single unemployment compensation payment in my life, even when I could legitimately have done so. Dad forgot that some people really did need the safety net of welfare or unemployment compensation or that the Fourteenth Street Protesters might look at things very differently if they had jobs. Early in life I developed the conviction: if you want to convert a Communist or any other adversary or exploiter of the system, help him be a capitalist.

The Irish-Americans were always active in the unions — partly because they were rebels, partly because they were manual workers. In *On the Waterfront*, it's no accident that Karl Malden's character is a priest. The Jesuits set up schools to train the union organisers. While I was generally sympathetic to the unionisation measures, one tactic that some of the renegades used appalled me, and I am sure would have appalled the priests too. The mounted cops were considered Cossacks, and some of the radicals would stuff their pockets with their kids' marbles and then spill them on the streets during mêlées with the cops, in order to trip the horses.

I was an active union member and proud that I was. The unions made a critical difference to the life of the dock-worker, making it much better than what my own father had experienced. I had a disability pension, and I had a job on the docks in which I didn't do any back-breaking work. Everything was agreeing with me, except my body.

In June 1948, I was on Pier 58 when a thirty-pound crate fell twelve feet from on top of a stack and smacked me in the head, knocking me unconscious. They didn't take me to the hospital. Instead I was treated in the medical facility on site. The following autumn, something more alarming happened — I was admitted to the Medical Arts Centre Hospital, for dark blood-caked stool, feeling weak and miserable. I was afraid that these were after-effects of both the 1948 accident and the 1939 one. In 1951, they treated me in Roslyn Park Hospital after I had a dizzy spell on the trolley tracks. I was nearly on my way to becoming human hamburger.

Then on 9 June 1952, I was standing on Pier 58 doing my job. Suddenly, I heard some people hollering, but I didn't realise that it was at me. An open-bed truck with stake sides was coming up behind me. One of the stakes was protruding outward. When the guys yelled to warn me, the truck was about 15 feet away. I turned the wrong way. Had I turned the right way, I would have seen it. The stake clobbered me on the right side of the head, neck, and shoulders.

Down I went. They brought me — unconscious and bleeding — to the first-aid room and then, when I tasted blood in my mouth, to the hospital. The diagnosis: concussion of the spinal cord, cervical level. I had broken two bones in my neck.

Almost five months later, the US exploded the first hydrogen bomb in the Marshall Islands, but what was going on in my head was about as catastrophic and damn near as loud!

Teddy Gleason thought it might be time for me to find a new workplace and I wholeheartedly agreed with him. I was wearing a ring brace around my neck that resembled the nose cone of Flash Gordon's rocket ship. I wasn't cut out for the fight game. The navy didn't want me. The fire department gave me my walking papers. And now it looked as though I was finished on the docks, too. The lesson I was about to learn was who is in charge of your self-confidence when all else fails.

5

The Widow's Broker (1951–62)

Al's recovery from the dock injury was much slower than his bounce back from the fire department accident. He was without the support of peers and feared that he would now be a life-long invalid and a burden on his young family. Having taken life-insurance sales courses, Al got his insurance broker's licence in 1951, and began to sell insurance for Canada Life. In 1954, another cycle of health problems beset him. Constant stress weakened his immune system and triggered bleeding ulcers; a massive haemorrhage was remedied only by multiple transfusions.

Al sued for damages for the dock injury. In 1955, a jury awarded him a substantial settlement, giving him $60,000 net. This nest-egg, soundly invested, combined with his pension, could have secured a solid lifetime income for a blue-collar worker, but Al wanted more from life.

He discovered that he had a gift for salesmanship. In pivotal encounters with the senior partner in a workingman's stock brokerage firm, Al the customer invested $50,000 in mutual funds; and Al the salesman succeeded in selling the senior partner himself a life-insurance policy. He was hired by the firm in 1955, and became a certified stock broker. Very quickly, he started to earn significant income. In 1957, at the age of 42, he bought a red Corvette for cash, having made a major sale. He continued to sell both mutual funds and insurance and instituted breakthrough training courses for female clients, aiding them with investment strategy. Having identified a need for mutual fund sales in marketing to mature women, he earned the moniker of the Widow's Broker. In 1956, Al took his first Dale Carnegie course in persuasion and public speaking. His successes were rewarded by a promotion to General Manager. Increasingly though he yearned for independence, and a row with the owner's son put him on the beach in the Caribbean in 1962.

'Your Honour, we have reached a judgment. We award the plaintiff $110,000.'

The judge at the New York Supreme Court screwed up his face. 'Mr Foreman, would you please approach the bench?' he asked with a blend of impatience and subdued amusement.

'Mr Foreman,' he continued in a lower voice. 'I appreciate the jury's enthusiasm as to their findings in this case, but I would like to remind the jury that you cannot award a plaintiff more damages in a civil suit than the plaintiff has sued for.'

Forty-five years later, that's the best I can reconstruct what happened in the courtroom that day in 1955. I sued the dock firm that caused the accident. The firm wanted to appeal. So I ended up taking eighty grand. After I paid the lawyers, I had sixty grand left, which was the equivalent of twenty years of pay, tax-free.

A truck had sailed by and part of its frame whacked me right in the back of the neck. My case was that the stake on the truck should never have hit me. When the suit went to trial in 1955, my three kids ranged in age from eight to eleven. During the three years preceding the trial, they didn't much care that Daddy looked like he was in a spacesuit. There was no way they didn't want to play with Daddy or learn how to throw a football as well as I could. But it hurt like hell. The pain was searing; but heck it was just muscle ache — it didn't break anything that hadn't already been broken.

A great pre-trial examination preceded the courtroom events. As I prepared to testify, my lawyer demanded that I tell him the totally candid, unvarnished truth. 'You tell me your answer, and I'll tell you how to phrase it,' he said.

He warned me that I would be viciously examined, questioned about my sex life, and accused of being an outstanding fake. He asked had I ever seen any small delivery trucks parked in front of the house and told me they were probably investigators taking pictures of me wrestling with my kids, playing football, and climbing ladders. In every respect, he was right.

They asked if I had ever been on a ladder doing minor work on the house. Had I had the brace on? I explained that I had taken it off because I couldn't work. I added that I was very sorry I had because it hurt like hell. When they asked about the kids, I lost my patience at one point and said, '[Before the accident], I could play with my kids ... I could play ball with them, I could go out with them. And now you try to do it, I've tried to do it, but it don't work so good. You just can't do it. If you have a kid ten or eleven years old and he wants to go to the cub scouts on Fathers' Night, and you can't go, he looks to his mother [and asks, "Is he ever going to get better?"]'

They challenged my work ethic. Why did I retire on full disability from the fire department, and not long afterwards start working as a checker on the docks? They didn't care that I was in a job that required walking around with a clipboard and a pencil.

My wife was scared to death of any legal proceeding, but she proved to be my best witness. On the stand, she shed honest tears for a man who was very proud of his physical strength, and now had a hard time sitting in a chair or enduring the vibrations on our wood floors.

In litigation, I have found the best advice is not to conceal what you did but to be able, with proper preparation, to explain what you did, with credibility, in public.

Even before the 1952 dock injury, Teddy Gleason got hold of me and told me to go back to school. My first step was to complete high school, through what in the US is called a GED — a high-school diploma for adults. 'Roach, why are you limiting yourself?' he kept nudging me further. 'Go learn real estate or insurance. You'll make ten times the money.'

I started to study things I could use immediately, like selling insurance. Most people focus in on a degree or a major. For me, it was what skill I needed next — from how to construct a sales call to how to remember people's names. It wasn't one simple discipline, but it all seemed to fit together.

Many evenings Dorothy would hop in the car and drive me to courses, or I would take the train. More times than I care to remember, I would get home at midnight, having fallen asleep on the Long Island Railroad and had to back-track home or have Dorothy come to pick me up.

Teddy Gleason wasn't talking just about education when he spoke to me about limits. He was talking about attitude as well. He was the first person to warn me that I was imposing limits upon myself and that this was dangerous. I was crippling my potential more than any injury or illness could. I had sentenced myself to life as a blue-collar working stiff, just as I had earlier fashioned myself into a tough guy and had to live *down* to all the self-limiting expectations that govern the tough-guy role — rejecting education, ignoring diplomacy, and scoffing at people who had the style and the know-how to play in the really big leagues.

The recovery from the Pier 58 accident was much harder than coming back after the World's Fair injury. Outside my family, no one gave a damn. The fire-fighting fraternity wasn't there to help me piece things back together again, to drive me to rehabilitation sessions or to cheer me on in my progress. If my career had put me on the docks first and in the fire department second, I doubt I would have made it. So many skills I had acquired in recovering from the first accident enabled me to come back from the more difficult circumstances surrounding the neck injury. I didn't know it when I was jumping rope and jogging as a training boxer, but doctors are convinced that the stamina and conditioning I developed as a boxer allowed me to survive my 1939 and 1952 accidents and probably a good deal more.

Off Your Feet and On Your Own

When injury or serious illness immobilises you, keeping your morale and motivation high can require tremendous diligence and planning. Here are several simple techniques that have served me well:

- *Don't wait for the cavalry to rescue you.* It's fine if you have people to help, but making the absence of help your excuse only hurts you.

- *Establish a minimum routine* of activity or exercise and stick to it with a vengeance, no matter how difficult or distracting a particular day may be.

- *Talk to yourself* and don't give a damn what people may think! Even today, when my back is killing me, you'll hear me say, 'C'mon, old buddy, you can make it!' as I manoeuvre my way in and out of a car. You know what, he generally does.

- *Plan ahead now.* Do you think you might some day be seriously ill or injured, and forced into a lengthy convalescence? The odds are high you will be. You need a reservoir of strength, not just to be healthy, but to tackle adversity when you aren't.

For a time, I worked as an independent insurance agent for Canada Life. I had obtained my New York State Insurance Broker licence in 1951. My father died in August 1952, two months after my neck injury on Pier 58, and it was a very emotional experience. To me Dad had seemed immortal; I didn't believe he would die. He was very strong and never really sick. This was a guy I had seen limp to work with a busted kneecap in a cast. It was turning the vivid memories of my father and his experiences into a persuasive appeal that enabled me to sell insurance. I recalled my youth.

I'm about twelve, I'm doing my homework one evening. My mother says, 'I'm going to lie down. Tell your father his dinner is on the back of the stove.'

It's a big Thatcher stove. Dad is tired when he comes in at about 8.30. He lies down on the couch and says, 'Pull off my workboots, Brother.'

I do. I can smell his socks. I can also smell a beer or two on his breath. It doesn't bother me. In fact, I will cherish it as a memory. He stares off into the floral curtains, deep in thought for several minutes, and then says quietly, 'I only wish that I could live long enough to raise you all.'

Many nights, I lay awake thinking about his comment: 'What's going to happen to us ... to all these kids, if Dad dies? Maybe Mom could work outside scrubbing floors or cleaning house, but what exactly would happen if he died?'

The insurance course said that selling insurance had to register with the prospect personally, but I had to dig deep in my own memory to make that idea meaningful. When I was growing up in Gerritsen Beach, the insurance agent would catch my father on a Saturday afternoon. He would regale him with the merits of a ten- or twenty-thousand dollar policy. My father would listen, and then wave him out of the living room, saying 'Get on with yeh. You must think I'm one of them movie stars like Tom Mix.'

Dad never bought an insurance policy, because no one

ever approached him in a way that he could relate to. Unwittingly, the insurance agent sentenced me — a twelve-year-old — and my mother and brothers and sisters to a life of fear because he *didn't know how to sell.*

Had the insurance salesman presented his argument to my father this way, what a difference it would have made: 'Mr Roach, for less than two buckets of ice cream, I can assure you that your youngest child could finish high school. Two buckets a week, Mr Roach. Think about it.'

Dad bought a lot of ice cream. He would have understood those dimensions. And he would have acted on them.

Never assume that the *biggest* number is
the one that people will listen to.

Holy moly, did that insurance story hit home! Canada Life held a big seminar in Toronto. I was asked to give a talk and I repeated my childhood experiences. Then I went further and said with anger, 'I accuse the insurance industry of a lack of awareness and urgency in not equipping agents to sell insurance. You aren't giving us the products we need. With the right products, selling would be simple. Your failings may not be on your conscience, but they should be. I've been in the shoes of that twelve-year-old, worried about what might befall the family should something happen to the breadwinner.'

After my talk, a Canada Life executive came to my table and offered me $16,000 a year just to make that same speech once or twice a month. It was tempting. The fire department pension, the investment earnings, the lawsuit settlement, and two speeches a month. That would be a respectable income. I thought about it for a minute, emptied my stein of Molson's Lager, wiped the foam off my lips with the back of my hand, and said, 'No dice.'

Some powerful feeling in my gut said that doing the same speech again and again like a carnival roadshow would make it too easy for me. My father's situation was the basis of a powerful lesson, but I couldn't commercialise it by repeating the same talk. However, the experience revealed that I *could* be imposing, talking in front of a group — and this without any formal training.

Three small kids were a handful. One of the older neighbours in Flatbush once commented to Dorothy, 'Mrs Roach, you have a lovely family, but we never see your husband.' Dorothy explained that I left for work early in the morning and attended night courses at the local college.

The neighbour looked heavenward in a rapture. 'Thank God every night for such a man,' she intoned, emphasising each point with her index finger. 'Never allow him to take out the garbage. Never allow the children to annoy him when he's studying, because when you're 40 — which is just around the corner — you'll be driving a Cadillac and wearing a mink, and your children will be in college.'

When my wife told me the good news, I aimed for the top shelf: 'No more garbage' is a good beginning; and, by the way, I don't cut lawns any more either.

As to the daily chores, I won my concessions. Kids from the neighbourhood cut grass and shovelled snow, until our own were old enough to do it. But my wife was still after me to paint the kitchen. One Saturday, I meant to see a guy about an insurance policy. Striving to be the dutiful husband, I left a phone message postponing the meeting, went to Sears and bought a couple of gallons of paint. With my back and neck in the shape they were, I spent the weekend in agony. My painting wasn't that great either.

On Monday, I ran into the client with whom I had delayed the meeting. He had never got the message, figured

I wasn't coming, and called up my competitor to give him the business instead. A $300 commission on a $10,000 insurance policy sailed out the window for the $30 it would have cost to bring in some guy to paint the kitchen!

Stretch Others to Stretch Yourself

When I'm in a hotel, I'll tell a colleague 'Let the concierge handle that.' Some out-of-shape scientist will be struggling with a bag, and I'll say, 'Give that to the bellman. I need your brains not your body.' My housekeeper will say that she's not sure she can do all of the ironing in one afternoon, and I'll remind her, 'That's what they have laundry services for.'

I owe a considerable amount of my vitality to renting a limo instead of a cab, or insisting that a restaurant rearrange seating in a tight rectangle, instead of an endless single row — how can you have an intelligent business conversation when guests must communicate by carrier pigeon?

All this I will do. But, never, do I ask for extra help and then lean back and enjoy the ride, nor do I ever let any of my colleagues indulge themselves. When you ask for special treatment, you have to rise to the occasion yourself. If you act like you deserve special services, you have to prove that you're worth putting out for and work that much harder.

I never painted another room. Painting your home can cost you plenty, I learned. My hearing loss was remarkable when I heard people comment within earshot of my wife: 'Ain't he a great guy? He's refurbishing the whole house.'

I hope he does a super job, I'd think, because all both of you are likely to see of the world is inside those four walls.

In 1954, not long before I turned 39, and about two years after my father died, I was feeling dizzy and faint and decided to see Dr Millet in Hempstead, who had been my physician since the time of the dock accident. While at his office, I started passing stool with black blood and then vomiting blood. I haemorrhaged so badly, I passed out. An ambulance rushed me to Nassau Hospital. Bleeding ulcers were diagnosed; in all, eight blood transfusions were pumped into me. They operated and removed about two-thirds of my stomach. During most of May, I was in and out of the hospital, and when in the hospital, I drifted in and out of consciousness. This time my brush with death was even closer. During one bleeding episode, my eyes were open and I could hear, but I was too weak to talk or move. Two doctors were conferring at my bedside, as the orderly rigged up another container of plasma. He shook his head and said, 'Seems like a stupid waste of blood, doesn't it...?' I recovered. It was slow, and I think part of the motivation was to take a poke at the orderly who was prepared to write my death notice. Thank goodness I never found him.

Assuming that I survived my medical adversity, what would I do with the proceeds of the litigation settlement? The dilemma lingered with me. I went to my banker and asked him to buy me $60,000 worth of government bonds. He told me I was out of my mind. He said to put the dough in stocks, but I was still very sceptical about stocks. This was less than thirty years after the great stock-market crash, and I refused to take that kind of risk. (My parents were still stuffing their savings in a mattress at that time.) Instead of buying individual stocks, I invested in a mutual fund, buying $50,000 worth of Fundamental Investors, and speaking directly with Mr Edwards of the Hempstead brokerage firm of Edwards & Hanly. I chose them because they specialised in brokerage work for the average joe, with a growing number of branch locations, and office hours in the evenings and on Saturday.

Communicating with the Comatose

Having been written off as a goner more than four times, I consider myself something of an expert on the exit gate from this world, and I have some conclusions to offer.

- The hospitalised person can hear what you say and sense what you do. When I overheard myself written off as a waste of blood transfusions, I was determined to survive, if only to kick the bastard in the shins for his remark. If exasperation can do that, think what being loved and cared for can do for a recovery. On two occasions, I have sent large, fragrant floral bouquets to young victims of catastrophic accidents. Both were in comas, both survived, and both remembered the distinctive aromas as stimuli that helped reawaken their senses.

  People who spend hours in intensive care talking to loved ones are not performing monologues for vegetables.

- During my ulcer ordeal, and in a similar but unrelated incident many years later, I experienced being in a long hall, and seeing my father waving his arms at me and shouting, 'Brother, go back! Go back!' Maybe he wanted to enjoy the peace and quiet up there just a little longer!

  People in comas take their cues from both sides of the boundary-line between life and death.

While I was with Mr Edwards, I sold *him* an insurance policy. He said that he wanted any guy who could turn the tables on him. 'How would you like to work in this business?' he asked. 'Mutual funds are the coming thing, and you'd be a natural for them.'

Bert Edwards, the senior partner, was a great-looking guy, stylishly stout. They called him the Silver Fox. He was a fantastic salesman — not just brokerage, but Miami land deals and even used cars. You name it. Old man Edwards was a fabulous closer and a shrewd gamesman. He was a fountain of encouragement. When you closed a million-dollar deal, he would come over and slap you on the back. I remember him saying so often, 'Roach, I could never have done as well as that. It will be a long time before any of us can top that.'

When he knew that a sell was iffy, he would barge in about two-thirds through the transaction and comment in an off-hand way: 'Well, you're in good hands. Roach is one of the finest investment brokers we have. I've never seen a guy take care of clients with more conscience and intelligence than he does.'

At golf, Edwards had an endless supply of wagering opponents because he was smart enough never to win by more than one putt. An imposing bridge player, he could memorise every hand.

I asked the finance guy at Edwards & Hanly if Bert was serious about hiring me. He said he sure was and that I was to start at a salary of $12,000 a year. I told him I preferred not to get a salary but to be paid on commissions. 'Naw, we don't give commissions,' he answered. 'We're like a big family.'

I stared him in the eye and said, 'I know what big families are like. I come from one. Four brothers. Four sisters. Nine pieces for the kids. More equal than they should sometimes be. If you want me, it will be on commission.' And, commission it was.

They say I revolutionised the New York investment firm of Edwards & Hanly. I'm credited with trailblazing the volume sales of mutual funds. In less than a year, they honoured me as the top producer, and I was featured in the national brokers' magazine — the first person to sell $2 million in mutual funds.

Having had so many serious injuries, I had lived with dire predictions that I would never make it to age forty. So when I turned forty-two in August 1957, I went out and bought a beautiful red Corvette for $4,500 after making a big sale. The firm's commission system was structured to yield potentially fantastic returns. If, for example, you sold $2 million of funds, you got $60,000 — sixty grand extra! I was going to make it while I could.

One of the heads of a big mutual fund sparked my curiosity one day. 'Roach,' he said, 'with your sales ability, if you ever attended the Dale Carnegie programme on speaking and leadership, you'd be unstoppable.' (Dale Carnegie was probably the foremost authority on public speaking and personal presence. His books remain best-sellers today worldwide.)

At first, I was insulted by the suggestion that I, one of the top investment salesmen in the country, should go to Dale Carnegie to learn to do *really well* what I was already doing well. But, I went — for the basic course in 1956 and the advanced course in 1958.

After the second session, I remember sitting in my living room shaking my head and wondering to myself 'How the hell did I ever sell before ?'* I had no idea of the system, the steps. By God, did they work! Dale Carnegie actually featured me in their advertisements. Even today when people ask me what I do, I say that I'm a salesman foremost, and I say it with pride. Today, it's hard to count

---

* Napoleon Hill's *Think and Grow Rich* was another important influence.

the number of people in my companies who have attended Dale Carnegie, and that includes science PhDs and executive officers. Dale Carnegie is not about selling spark plugs or semiconductors — it's about selling yourself.

Dealing on Wall Street, I learned a lot about investor psychology and human psychology. For example, when a broker picks up a telephone, and the client on the other end says, 'Hey, Roach, remember that stock you sold me...', that means it just went down, and you hold the telephone receiver at arm's length to hear the rest of the story. If it's 'Hey, Roach, remember that stock *I bought...*', you can bet it just went up .

In eight years on the Exchange, I had maybe three reneges, where a customer demanded that a trade be rescinded. When the customer insisted, the customer was right, and the trade was undone. I still smile over one busted deal. A customer wanted to buy some shares of Texas Instruments. He told me to buy it, but he didn't specify the price. During the day, the stock jumped from 9 to 10. When the customer got the mailed confirmation, he exploded. He said it was worth no more than 9, and demanded that we cancel the sale. 'Hold onto the trade, the stock will go back up again,' I advised.

'No, break the trade!' the customer insisted. We kept the stock and put it into what brokers call the 'error account', where it promptly climbed to 40.

Bulls and bears make money. Greedy pigs go to the slaughterhouse. Generous people, plain and simple, tend to be more successful than greedy ones, *especially* when the name of the game is making money.

I was the first person in the firm ever to run an investment advisory seminar for women. We expected twenty women, and over three hundred signed up. We had to relocate the meeting from Hempstead to the Garden City Hotel. Most brokers were so damn dumb! They didn't realise how much money women, especially widows, controlled. My philosophy was: *don't cast for fish in the desert!*

I was also among the first to appoint female brokers and send them to school. The owner's son said to me, 'Roach, are you insane? They'll probably go to bed with the customers.'

'Don't let your mother hear that,' I replied. 'She's in the first class.'

I left the industry in 1962, and twenty years later I would meet women who would tell me that their $200,000 was now worth $2 million. When I put them into mutual funds, I got only one commission rather than earning commissions on each trade, but the volume of business was enormous. So many times, widows would beg me to help get rid of brokers pestering them to buy this or sell that. 'When my husband was alive, he loved it,' they would lament. 'It gave him somebody to talk to. But, I can't stand this muttonhead calling me up and prattling on about dividends and diversification.'

At Edwards & Hanly, I became known as 'The Widow's Broker' and was a relentless advocate of widow power. My management of the investment account of one particular widow, for whom I'll use the pseudonym 'Mrs LaFarge' (which bears no resemblance to the name of anyone I have ever met), catapulted me to success. Mrs LaFarge was somewhat younger than her surgeon husband. The venerable Dr LaFarge was not only a nimble surgeon, he was also a real hotshot at choosing stocks. He loved to pick 'em. I just executed his orders. When Dr LaFarge checked out to the Big Operating Room in the Sky, he was worth about three million bucks.

This was back in the 1960s, when $3 million was real money.

About a month after he died, Mrs LaFarge appeared in my office with a dark veil and prim, high-collar widow's weeds. 'Al,' she said with a tear in her eye and a crack in her voice, 'on his deathbed my husband made me promise that I would come to you and request you do for me exactly what you did for him. So, I'm here to ask you to do that.'

'Wait a minute. *Do what?* How can I execute orders if I don't know what stocks to buy and sell.' She looked totally crestfallen. Trying to make her feel better, I offered to buy and sell what the company recommended.

'OK, do that,' Mrs LaFarge said. But, as I thought about it, I just couldn't inflict that on a defenceless widow. Some brokerage companies have been known to tout stocks that it may be more in their interest to sell than in their customers' interests to buy.

I circled back with another question, 'What *exactly* did your husband say you should do?'

'"Go to Al Roach,"' she recited like a girl in a school play and added, '"Don't argue with him. Do what he tells you to do."'

'W-e-l-l, that's not what you said before,' I sighed with relief. 'But I think I understand now what the doctor would wish me to attempt. What kind of money do you need to live at the style to which you have been accustomed?'

'Three or four thousand dollars a month.'

'What?' I roared.

'If that's too much...' she gulped in a panic.

'No, no,' I assured her and suggested it would probably be best if we backed our calculations up and started from scratch.

'Al, what kind of income do *you* think I should expect?' she asked.

'About 6 per cent net on your investments. That's roughly $180,000 a year, which is about $3,500 a week.'

Above: Me with my eight brothers and sisters who survived into adulthood. This picture was taken in Brooklyn in 1947 at the celebration of my parents forty-fifth wedding anniversary. I'm fourth from the right in the back row.

Left: My wife Dorothy and I had our first date on 25 May 1941, on her eighteenth birthday. Our three children were born between 1943 and 1947.

Above: On our arrival in Buffalo, New York in 1963, where I became CEO of International Breweries. (*L to R*), my son AP, my daughter Dorothy, my wife Dorothy, myself, my mother Nellie, and my son Tim.

Left: Bessie, the firehouse mascot for Engine Company 310, was renowned as a great watchdog and for her many litters of puppies.

Below: My sister Margaret in her Dominican habit and me, the Fireman, in uniform.

Above: Some of the Men of Engine 310. I'm second from the left. Their support and encouragement after my back accident was key to my recovery.

Above: The Fire Department ladders raised at the 1939 World's Fair Demonstration. A 35-foot ladder was stretched across the top of these to stage the jump into the waiting net. After 23 successful landings, I broke my back on attempt 24.

Above: Daughter Dorothy and son AP on my back. Out of the Fire Department and working as a checker on the docks. I seem concerned about the future, don't I?

Right: At age 82 with my great-grandson Robbie, a live wire like the old man.

The Mohawks make me a Blood Brother and an honorary chief in 1964. On my Certificate of Adoption — one of the greatest honours I have ever received — my Indian name translates as *Man of Action*.

Above: Drawing a frosty pitcher of suds. My grandfather once owned a string of taverns in New York City.

Below: The fleet of White Mustangs arrives at Iroquois headquarters. Adorned with Indianhead emblems, at times they made some of our sales reps more recognisable than they wanted to be.

Left: Receiving the 'Freedom of Niagara' award from Mayor E. Dent Lackey of Niagara Falls, New York, August 1965.

Right: TII opens its new headquarters in Copiague in 1971. I'm third from the left. To my right is Dorothy Conboy, my loyal administrative aide for many years. My wife Dorothy is to her right. Cutting the ribbon is Dan Lundvall, then President of TII.

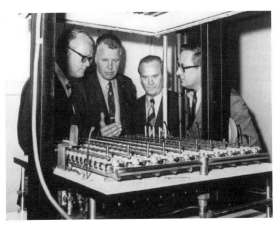

Left: Inside the new plant, we look at models of surge-protection equipment. From left to right, Congressman Jim Grover, Dan Lundvall, myself, and the late Congressman Jack Wydler. Over the years, Jim and Jack spearheaded a number of legislative initiatives for us.

Top: Observing a class during my Wall Street days as a manager for the investment firm of Edwards & Hanly.

Left: TII managers at our Toa Alta plant in1980. *Rambo* Roach is third from right. José Ramon Garcia ('Dominic') is third from the left and Greg Cortes is on the right.

Below: The American Stock Exchange welcomes TII to its trading floor. To my right are a representative of the Stock Exchange and my son Tim, now President of TII.

Opposite: In 1983 *Forbes* declared me an 'Up & Comer' at the age of 68.

Forbes

Volume 132, Number 12   November 21, 1983

The Up & Comers ·

Al Roach has come a long way from a boyhood of street fighting and a boxing career in the Army.

Up from Harlem

By John A. Byrne

ALFRED ROACH, a plucky, self-made Irish-American born in Harlem 68 years ago, figures he's sitting pretty these days. Roach, chairman of TII Industries, thinks that he will be able to sell more of his telecommunications gear to the Bell System after AT&T's breakup next year.

"Once that umbilical cord is cut from Western Electric"—now the biggest supplier of equipment to Bell companies—"they are going to be the most independent guys you've ever seen in your life," he says. "I've got a feeling we're going to do a lot more selling."

Roach has to be taken seriously. Even against Western Electric, he has done a superior job of selling his overvoltage protectors—tiny devices that protect telephones, computers and other electronic equipment by grounding sudden "spikes" in voltage. During the past decade more than 40% of the company's sales came from AT&T's operating companies.

TII, based in Copiague, N.Y., experienced one of its few setbacks this year, when it reported a loss for the first time since it went public in 1968. The loss came mainly from a $2.8 million inventory writeoff, a big one for a company with yearly sales of only $23.4 million. Roach asserts that the writeoff was made necessary by a supplier's failure to ship acceptable parts, and TII is suing the supplier for $10 million. Until this year TII had averaged a return on equity of more than 20% over the preceding five years. Its balance sheet shows $4 million in cash and no debt.

In any case, Roach seems perfectly competent to manage his problem. "My friend," he tells a visitor to his modest office, "you didn't survive in Harlem unless you could run like hell or fight like hell, and my legs are too short. I had to fight my way out."

And so he did, in the manner of his boxer father. Roach joined the Army and held its welterweight boxing title in 1934 and 1935. After leaving the Army he lurched from job to job for years, working as a merchant marine, a life insurance salesman, a stockbroker and a consumer moneylender. At one point he managed the ailing Iroquois brewery in upstate New York.

Not until the early 1960s did Roach find his true calling. No college graduate, he still had become a voracious reader of technical magazines. In one of them, he read of a British maker of a gas tube that better protected new transistor telephones from lightning and power surges. Sensing an opportunity, he crossed the Atlantic and paid $60,000 in cash to

TII Chairman Alfred Roach
A high-voltage act.   Photo by Joyce Ravid

Right: The Hon. Carlos Romero-Barceló, Governor of Puerto Rico 1976–84 (left), was the first former governor of Puerto Rico to serve in Congress. We worked together on the Caribbean Basin Initiative launched by President Reagan.

Left: Senegal's President Léopold Senghor, the first native African member of the French Academy, as well as a great statesman, appointed me Honorary Consul to the Republic of Senegal. Here we shake hands at a black-tie Washington function.

Right: Dr Jonas Salk, the man who conquered polio and one of the greatest scientists of our time, reviews his plans for the future with me at a World Academy of Arts and Sciences meeting in Minneapolis in 1994.

Above: At a meeting with Ronald Reagan in 1987, the President shook my hand in appreciation of what I had done to help spearhead national interest in superconductivity.

Below: George Bush shakes my hand at the White House. It was in his adopted state of Texas, at the University of Houston, that many superconductivity breakthroughs took place.

Right: Second from left is Prof. Sir John R. Vane, who won the 1982 Nobel Prize for Medicine for discovering aspirin's mechanism of action. To my right is Prof. Gustav Born, whose father Max won the Nobel Prize in 1954. On the left is Prof. Ciaran Regan of University College Dublin. Both Gus and Ciaran are on ABS's Advisory Board.

Left: Fr Theodore Hesburgh, an educational dynamo and a magnificent human being, was President of Notre Dame University in the US from 1952 to 1987.

Right: With Professor Michael Sela, W. Garfield Weston Professor of Immunology, Weizmann Institute of Science in Rehovot, Israel in 1994.

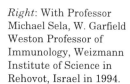

Above: American Biogenetic Sciences, Inc. Global Network Dinner at Dublin Castle, 11 August 1993. I'm at the centre of the photo and Dr Gus Born is to the right. The tall gentleman behind me is Professor Rem Petrov, Vice President of the Russian Academy of Sciences in Moscow and a member of ABS's Advisory Board. On the very right is Dr Emer Leahy who is now Senior Vice-President of Business Development.

Below: With then Taoiseach Albert Reynolds, having briefed him on the research projects undertaken by ABS in Ireland.

Above: With Mr Chen of the Environmental Protection Organisation and Mr Hong of the Shanghai School of Medicine, Beijing, 1979.

Left: Beside me is Prof. Lu Sheng Dong, Professor of Molecular Biology and Vice-President of the Chinese Academy of Medical Sciences. Seated are Prof. Denian Ba, Professor of Immunology, President of the Chinese Academy of Medical Sciences and Peking Union Medical College and Ellena Byrne, Executive Vice-President of ABS Global Network.

Above: Standing on the Great Wall, an experience at once energising and humbling.

Above: This 1993 dinner, attended by leading physicians and scholars, celebrated Irish medicine and extolled Ireland as a global centre for biotechnology excellence in the 21st century. On the left hand side of the table at the very back is Irish poet Brendan Kennelly.

Right: The day after prostate cancer surgery in 1987. Ten years have passed, and the genie seems safely back in the bottle.

Below: On a second visit to St Saviour's Gym in Dublin in June 1998, I repeated my message to the kids: Take care of your body today, and it will take care of you later when you need it.

Above: At the Berkeley Court Hotel in Dublin, I am looking at a painting of the Church of the Resurrection in St Petersburg. I had just acquired the painting in 1993. The reason I seem concerned may be my pensive Open Letter in the *New York Times* titled 'An Urgent Message To The Governments and Business Leaders of the G-7 Nations — Canada, France, Germany, Great Britain, Italy, Japan and the United States of America' in which I raise the need for the West to be aware of Russian economic instability during its transition to a market economy.

Below: On the threshold of Trinity College, Dublin, with great respect for the 'Celtic Tiger' and its ever-increasing role in the world's knowledge economy.

'Good Lord, I could never use up that much money.'

'Better get used to the idea,' I advised her.

Over time, she certainly learned to. She was a perfect candidate for the earliest generation of mutual funds, which were making their début at the time. That's exactly what I put her into. At first, she would see me twice a year. Steadily, her manner brightened, and her clothes — well, the price tags got higher and the necklines got lower. Then she discovered the Caribbean and the Mediterranean, and it was harder for her to find time to see me. I didn't mind at all. She was singing my praises to other New York widows in the cafés of St Tropez or on the sun decks of luxury liners steaming into the ports of Aruba and Curaçao. Mrs LaFarge taught me the power of word-of-mouth marketing.

The last time I met Mrs LaFarge was in front of Harry Winston's on Fifth Avenue. She was probably seventy at the time. 'Yoo hoo,' I heard someone warble behind me and turned around to see a woman draped in sable from head to toe, with a string of pearls so big that 'the oysters must have been kept working overtime', as they say. Behind the over-sized designer sunglasses was the Widow LaFarge being helped into her sleek new Mercedes by Francesco, a dashing young Italian chauffeur. Mrs LaFarge squeezed Francesco's bulging biceps as she swung into the back seat of the car. She smiled at me and said, 'You remember me, Al, don't you? How do you like my new ... *Everything*?' It was clear that not only had she learned to live up to a new style, but she was also well along in her post-doctoral studies!

I tried to bring my brand of Harlem/Brooklyn pragmatism to Wall Street, especially in the investments I selected. We would be approached by plenty of entrepreneurs, running small businesses and trying to raise capital to expand. In 1958, if I met a guy driving a 1946 Packard, I would say to myself, 'This is my kind of guy.'

On the other hand, there would be a company looking for $2 million, and the boss was driving a brand new Caddy; if I tried to phone him, I'd find that he was at lunch from 11.30 to 2.30; he somehow managed to fit his work week in between Tuesday and Thursday; and in a company presentation to outsiders like me, he would demean his associates with demoralising and degrading remarks. Such a company could be sure that none of the $2 million would ever be coming from my clients.

I was no expert on products. For that, I had to rely on engineering and marketing people. My ability was in judging the character of the people. On the whole, my assessment of the managers I saw in mainstream business was pretty low. 'If you're so smart,' my wife would say, 'why don't you find a company and run it yourself.'

'Maybe I will,' I'd reply. 'Maybe I will ... someday.'

The whole mentality on Wall Street began to offend me, which is saying a lot for someone steeped in the street-tough ways of Harlem, the army, the merchant marine, and the docks. When I recently read Michael Lewis's account of life on Wall Street, entitled *Liar's Poker*, it brought back some memories of my Wall Street days. 'If the market felt fidgety,' Lewis writes, 'if people were scared or desperate, [a given bond trader] herded them like sheep into a corner, then made them pay for their uncertainty. He sat on the market until it puked gold coins.' Later he describes selected customers who 'met the two requirements ... that they be small investors and, second, that they be so awed by Salomon Brothers as to assume anything they were told was good advice.'* That attitude permeated Wall Street and I had enough of it. As to the number of words beginning in 'f' and ending

---

* Lewis, Michael, *Liar's Poker: Rising Through the Wreckage on Wall Street*. New York: W.N. Norton & Company, Inc., 1989, pp. 88, 170.

in 'g', according to my wife, they hadn't gone down since my dock days; they were actually on the rise!

Successful stock deals had amassed enough for me to put all three kids through college. My stomach was certainly smaller and sure felt better after the operation (although mega-doses of cayenne pepper, herbologists advise me today, could have done a far better and faster job of eliminating the bacteria that are the actual cause of ulcers), but my heart wasn't in the brokerage business any longer. An almost sibling rivalry evolved between me and Mr Edwards' son and it blew up in 1962 into an irreversible situation after one large sale I made.

The opportunity arose to run a small bank in Puerto Rico. The bank, Key Finance Corp, was actually more of a loan company. There wasn't much work involved. My lifestyle was the envy of many — a little sailing, a bit of boating, a tad of banking, and a whole lot of beach. After all, it was time — *turn me over, please, I'm done on this side* — to prepare for my golden years.

6

A Man of Action (1962–65)

Rummaging through a dusty second-hand bookstore in London in the early 1960s, Al's wife discovered the advice of the Renaissance sage Luigi Cornaro, and insisted he read the book. It had a profound impact on his goals and long-term focus. From mid-1962 to mid-1964, Al commuted to and from New York to run a modest bank/consumer loan business in Puerto Rico. Knowing of his experience with unions, a small group of investors approached Al to become president of struggling International Breweries, headquartered in Buffalo, the home of Iroquois Breweries — International's flagship business.

In April 1964, Al reluctantly accepted the post of chairman, his first general management assignment outside the brokerage industry. In short order, he imposed drastic operating reforms, and struck an accord with a demanding union. He showed a knack for marketing, introducing new products, building important ties to minority communities, and raising bold challenges to competitors. The Indian Defense League of America adopted Al as a blood brother in the summer of 1964.

By September 1964, International Breweries was restored to profitability. The firm's stock moved steadily upward and attracted the attention of corporate raiders. Soon the company was locked in a bitter takeover campaign. The final battle was a complicated proxy struggle, which Al and his supporters lost. Offered the post of president under a new chairman, Al declined and left International Breweries in 1965. During his brief tenure, he became a highly visible member of the New York State business community. Financially, he benefited from the sharp rise in the stock's value. Al's family remained in suburban New York, while he commuted to work first in Puerto Rico and then Buffalo, and their home in Levittown was to be the proving grounds for his next career.

'...[A]n old man, even of a bad constitution, who leads a regular and sober life is surer of a long one than a young man of the best constitution who leads a disorderly life.'*

Those words come from an invigorating little book on the wise way to live life, by the Italian architect Luigi Alvise Cornaro, born in 1475. Cornaro lived to be ninety-one. Born with a lousy constitution, Cornaro abused his health further for the first forty years of his life by eating and drinking liberally. Then he noticed his friends were dying off, one by one, victims of their own lifestyles.

Luigi, *amico*, I'm listening, I said to myself. I was relaxing, sure enough, with my little bit of banking and my whole lot of beaching. Dorothy and I had taken the kids to the Caribbean. Otherwise, I was neglecting myself. I was overweight and had acquired the disagreeable habit of eight to ten fat cigars a day — not smoking them, but biting on them. Fortunately, I had never been a slave or even a companion to drink, but I remember towards noon one day, finishing a screwdriver and walking into the bathroom of our villa with a cigar in one hand and a safety razor in the other, unsure whether I should shave with the cigar and smoke the razor or vice versa. I had recently read in an article that an early sign of alcoholism was spiking the morning orange juice with vodka. With that, I made a career decision and took one look at Dorothy. 'Your husband is becoming an alcoholic,' I said. 'Pack up the kids and let's get the hell out of here.'

Not long before this, I had read Cornaro's book after my wife found it in a second-hand bookshop in London. It had quietly made an impression on me. I was approaching my fiftieth year. I had the fire department pension and the lawsuit nest-egg that had multiplied considerably

* Cornaro, Luigi, *How to Live One Hundred Years*, London: Health for All Publishing Company, 1959.

through my investments at Edwards & Hanly. I had all the financial equipment to hang up my spurs, and my body had been racked by enough injury and illness to make me a 'suitable candidate' for retirement. But keeping my embers at low heat was draining me; and my whole psyche seemed to recoil against the course I was following.

On the plane headed into JFK (John Kennedy had only recently been assassinated, and the airport had changed its name from Idlewild just months earlier) to take a look at a business opportunity, I took Cornaro's book out of my carry-on bag and began to reflect on some of the passages. Here were principles upon which I was prepared to alter my own lifestyle:

- *An old man with a bad constitution and the right disciplines had a better chance than a young man with a good constitution and bad habits.* What new hope this gave me! Cornaro's own life had been vivid proof of this truth. I vowed to compete on the same footing as a younger man and to show that my habits and personal will mattered more than either my condition or my age.

- *Always play with the youngest of your grandchildren.* I didn't even have any grandchildren yet, but I hoped that I would, and I prayed that I would one day play with my great-grandchildren, too. Further, I actively sought out younger acquaintances so that all my friends would not be in the same greying age range.

- *'... [W]hatever pleases the palate must agree with the stomach and nourish the body; or whatever is palatable must be equally wholesome and nourishing.'* Eat sensibly, I thought, and my mind drifted back to my youth when I had devoured corn and tomatoes raw off the vine at little farms on Long Island. How long had it been since I had bitten into a huge juicy Bartlett pear and experienced that succulent juice running down my face? So beautiful and light. My daily diet was going to change fast and recapture some of those cherished pleasures now passing me by.

* *'Eating little makes a man live very long, and living very long he must eat a great deal.'* More than the wisdom of portion control, this captured the rhythm and pacing of a distance runner. And a distance runner I was determined to be!

Cornaro's advice wasn't the sole building block in my new philosophy. I was later to add skills in stress management, breathing, body detoxification, nutrient supplementation, and stretching. The complete package has proved a powerful arsenal in stoking the fire in my belly and in making my life unexpectedly enjoyable for the past thirty years. My approach to dealing with life's temptations isn't the only one around, but it's the one that's worked for me.

The irony in my life at this particular time — as my mind was pulsing with images of wellness and personal reform — was the business opportunity I was travelling to consider. The jet was cruising back to New York so that I could fulfil every Irishman's dream. I had been chosen to run a major brewery.

While I was at Edwards & Hanly, I had impressed an unlikely trio of investors with my repertoire of skills. One of the trio was Chinese, one was Japanese, and the third was a scion of the Du Pont family, who was tragically killed in a private plane crash several years later. The three asked to meet with me. I was flattered. Here's my recollection of the conversation:

'We've found an investment,' they began. 'It's considerably under-priced versus its book value.'

'Sounds interesting,' I replied.

'Management of it would require intimate knowledge of unions.'

'Know unions like the back of my hand from my days in the Merchant Marine as an organiser, and on the docks as a checker.'

'This is one helluva tough environment,' they continued.

'Hell, I'm your man. I've been battling tough guys and winning ever since the nuns appointed me their chief bully fighter on the softball diamond of Resurrection Elementary School!'

'And, the job will really best be done by someone who is a native New Yorker, since the headquarters are in Buffalo.'

There was a deafening silence.

'Are you out of your frigging minds?' I finally managed to say.

For a New York City Catholic, going to Buffalo is like a heavy-duty sentence to Purgatory! Maybe worse. It is so cold in Buffalo that they celebrate summer with a picnic only in those years that it falls on a weekend. These guys wanted Captain Al to trade in his tropical paradise for a dogsled and an igloo.

'You'll at least take a look?' they asked innocently.

After an hour of intensive arm twisting I agreed that I *might* take a trip to Buffalo.

So, discomfort about having a too comfortable future finally got me on the aeroplane north to take a look at International Breweries. The flagship firm had been in business since 1847, and in 1963 the total corporation was doing over $25 million in sales on production of three million barrels. The firm had eight hundred employees. International owned Iroquois in Buffalo and other breweries in such towns as Findlay, Ohio, near Columbus, in Covington, Kentucky, near Cincinnati, and in Tampa, Florida.

Although I was still undecided whether to take the job, the *Buffalo Courier* played up that a Wall Street tycoon (I always thought typhoon fit better) was going to save the brewery. When I toured the plant, a little old fellow grabbed my hand and kissed it. He told me that he and his wife were praying for me and that they would light a candle every night. I knew I was dead. They had me. They had set me up to be their Messiah and I bit.

Days later, when I returned to Buffalo to take up my duties, two hundred Iroquois employees met me at the airport. The car that took my family and me downtown had a trailer hitched up to it. On it was — what else? — a huge stuffed buffalo.

Buying International Breweries cost plenty, but we knew the underlying assets were worth far more. We invested in a very thorough due diligence, which entails bringing in an outside auditor to review the books and practices, verifying that the books are correct and that the assets are properly valued. We found some practices we challenged. Several managers left the company. There was also an unhealthy climate. When you find that, you usually find corruption too.

At a plant-wide meeting, I announced that the rock had been overturned, and I was going to cut off the head of the snake I found under it. I emphasised that I knew plenty about unions and had even helped organise one. I told them that during my days on the docks, I had learned all the tricks about cradling a pallet, and worse. I assured them that we wouldn't set up a police state, but warned: 'If you eight hundred people want to keep your jobs, it's up to you. If you force us into bankruptcy, we'll suffer no monetary loss. In fact, we'll get our money back at a gain of three hundred per cent on the land sale. We paid three dollars a share to take over this brewery. We have since learned that the land beneath it is worth eleven dollars a share. If we have to, we'll declare bankruptcy and liquidate the business. If you're caught stealing, I have the union's agreement that you will lose union accreditation permanently and never work again as a member of that union. Finally, I need your help to work with me to nail the snake before the snake nails all of us.'

How to Fight Abuses
Inside an Organisation

- *Use the best outside resources.* Engage trained professionals to diagnose internal problems and map a course of action. It's easy for managers to fantasise about what's wrong and drive the inquiry off course, while losing valuable time.

- *Show you know.* Once people learn you're on to their little cons and that you can explain the details of how they were able to get away with murder in the past, you rekindle in them the fear of doing something wrong.

- *Shun police state thinking.* Police states try to make fear the number one motivator. While people should have a healthy fear of doing something wrong, they should harbour a far more favorable urge to do things right and well.

- *Declare an amnesty.* Encourage people to come forward and bare their chests. Restitution usually matters less than the deeply buried problems people will expose by coming forward. Otherwise, it will take you months longer to detect the real trouble. (Government tax authorities have known this for years.)

- *Deputise everyone.* Dramatise how abuses take money out of everyone's pockets and undermine each person's future. Enlist everyone's help to stamp out internal theft.

Four days later, late at night, I got an anonymous call that some hoods on the inside were going out with three trailer-loads of beer, selling it to our own distributors at half price. They had probably been playing this racket for years. We alerted the police, and the crooks were nabbed.

An image of me was being created around town, and one columnist who visited my office compared me to James Cagney, yelling questions to the staff and gesturing to beat the band.

Other things bothered me too. Sheer neglect was a problem. Paint was peeling from the ceiling. 'We make a product people consume,' I roared. 'They pour it inside themselves. This place should be immaculate!'

We began to clean the plant up, and you could see the effect on the people in their improved dress and in their morale when they came in for their shift.

The main shift started at 7.45, so I decided to begin my management meetings at 6.45. Guys who never talked with each other began to talk. Then the managers started to realise that they were a team. *I-need-you-and-you-need-me* looks shot around the table. They recognised that they shared the same problems, and were amazed to learn that they even had the same solutions in mind. When they argued, I loved it, because it proved they cared. The only rule was that they weren't allowed to say 'That's stupid' to someone else's idea.

'Prove that it's stupid,' I would say. 'And if you can't, get out.' I meant it. It's always better for managers to be challenged by their peers than by their bosses, and peers won't challenge each other when they fear being hounded or humiliated for their fresh ideas.

Straightening up management was only half the battle. The union was an equal or greater challenge. At the beginning, labour relations looked like smooth sailing. The union gave me a moratorium for two years: no strikes and no raises. Otherwise, at the first sign of life in the business, they would have marched in and demanded a raise that would have killed the company. By then, the unions were using lawyers and economists, and I hoped that union leadership would work together with me reasonably. I was wrong. Within three months, the union broke the agreement and campaigned for a 30 cent an hour raise.

'You're out of your mind,' I told them. 'I can't afford it.' Managers have to be clear, basic, and fearless when they negotiate with unions. They threatened to strike, and I said I would padlock the grounds and tear the buildings down for a parking lot if they did.

At a meeting, a smart-ass delegate started baiting me and tossing around obscenities. Women were there, and I told him to cut it out. When he swore at me personally, I threatened to break his jaw. We glared at each other, then the meeting cooled down. One of the more even-tempered union people explained that they couldn't stick by their agreement with me because another local of theirs had just signed a contract with a brewery in the South, in which the workers got a very meaty increase.

'You *can't* be serious,' I said. 'That mega-brewery is almost totally automated and produces ten million barrels a year. It employs only forty people, twenty-two of whom are truck-drivers. The rest are engineers and management. Only half of the forty are union. We, on the other hand, are labour-intensive. Our three breweries employ 860 people to produce just three million barrels. Do the arithmetic. Your thirty cents an hour will cost us about a million dollars and put us under. It's your choice, but it's hard to collect union dues from a parking lot.'

My message was simple: tie any future increases to the barrelage — the barrel output — of the breweries. If the southern brewery could afford to raise twenty people thirty cents an hour, that was $12,336 in added annual payroll expense to put ten million barrels through the door. If we were delivering only three million barrels, that gave me only $3,700.80 as a raise pool, assuming the same level of productivity. Dividing that among 860 people, meant $4.30 a year per person. Divide that number by 2,056, and you were talking about a pay increase of about one five-thousandth of a penny per hour. Talk of any wage increase was ridiculous. The union finally saw my point.

Don't assume people are stupid if they don't see things your way, especially if you don't bother to explain the reasoning behind your way.

At roughly the same time, the unions representing dock workers were using similar techniques. Containers were making handling obsolete on the docks, and it was clear that twenty-one-man teams would soon be three-person ones. The principle worked to the dock-workers' advantage because the dock-workers were willing to reduce their workforce substantially.

Iroquois Industries was my first excursion into the world of corporate racial diplomacy. Fierce race riots hadn't yet beset Detroit and Los Angeles. Martin Luther King was still alive. No one appreciated the racial time bomb that America was sitting on. Buffalo had a sizeable African American population, and that was reflected in both our workforce and our customer base. The Harlem I grew up in thrived on tolerance. Prejudice was foreign to my nature. And it just made good business sense to draw African Americans into the business.

We became a sponsor of one of the first African American beauty pageants. And in a move with far greater community and strategic significance, I nominated football player Ernie Warlick of the Buffalo Bills to the board of directors. To my knowledge, he was the first African-American on the board of an American Stock Exchange company. A graduate of North Carolina College, and an Air Force veteran, he contributed first-rate brainpower to the board.

What Intelligent Race Relations Really Take

Respect: Give people the opportunity to compete for excellence.

Respect: Prove that acting responsibly is also good business.

Respect: Treat the leaders of a community comparably to the leaders of a nation.

Respect: Be aware of problems on the horizon and act to defuse them before they become full-scale crises.

Even at that time, there would be sporadic neighbourhood property damage to buildings belonging to factory owners targeted as racist or exploitative. A couple of minority community leaders came up to me one day and told me not to worry. Because of the honest and visible efforts we were making, we were on the *don't touch* list.

From day one, I loved to get involved in Iroquois's marketing programme, and we managed some novel achievements. Our print and television ads featured a very attractive Indian *squaw*. The model who performed the role was the wife of the marketing director. She was beautiful, convincing — and 100 per cent Polish, a member of the Polish Tribe along the Vistula as I recall! Jack Kemp, who went on to become 1996 Republican Vice-Presidential candidate in the United States, played for the Buffalo Bills during my tenure at Iroquois, and he did some appearances for us.

My personal promotion of the product was endless. I landed at the football stadium in a helicopter during a Buffalo Bills game. I challenged the heads of the other big breweries to a taste test: ten thousand dollars to the brewmaster who could tell their brand from ours. I still believe to this day that beer is beer, and it is very hard to distinguish the taste of different brands.* My extra advantage was that I also knew that the colder beer was chilled, the harder it was to distinguish its taste. Unfortunately, I never got to put my secret weapon to work because no competitor ever accepted the challenge. Maybe they knew the same secret I did.

We could see the market shifting towards premium beers, so we developed a new upscale brand called Tomahawk Ale. The packaging was classy, with silver foil around the cap. An Indian overlooked a crystal clear lake, suggesting the purity of the water we were using. The malt content was higher than that of our main competitor. (My brewmaster told me that if the alcohol content moved any higher, we'd have to register and sell it as wine.) Then I launched a word-of-mouth campaign that this was the most powerful aphrodisiac money could buy. If a lady sipped a glass of this brew, it could rocket a gentleman's love life into earth orbit. Guys would steal up to me and whisper into my ear, 'You know what I heard about this beer and its — er, you know — *side-effects*? Well, yes-sir-ee, let me tell you it is *true*, and then some!'

I would smile appreciatively and look like I didn't understand what in the world they were talking about.

To pep up the sales force, I went out and bought thirty

---

* When a competitor had a fire once, we honoured the ancient brewery tradition and brewed their beer for them. I went ballistic. 'Won't they have to disclose their secret formula to us?'

Our brewmaster laughed over his shoulder at me, as he walked down the hall. 'Mr Roach,' he said, 'beer is beer.'

white Mustangs, Lee Iacocca's biggest success story at
Ford. We had the Iroquois Indian stencilled on the sides,
the hood, the roof and the trunk. All the salesmen were
enormously proud of their coupés. The emblem looked like
the insignia on a police car. These babies were sleek ...
and noticeable. Noticeable indeed. My head of sales called
me one day and told me to meet him at an address on
64th Street. When I arrived at the address, it turned out
to be a topless bar. Seventeen Iroquois Mustangs were
parked outside. It was during office hours. They were
having a tête-à-tête with the big titties, and most of these
guys were so shameless *they weren't even drinking our
brand!* When the manager of the place saw me, he recognised me from the newspaper photos, and the blood
drained from his face. I asked him if he knew who the
Iroquois salesmen were. He nodded.

I gave him twenty bucks and told him to go around silently and set a bottle of Iroquois beer in front of each of
them. 'Make sure the label is facing them,' I growled
quietly.

One by one, as each bottle was plonked down, they
started to look around, first at each other, and then they
caught sight of me. They cowered like a bunch of school-
children who had been exposed for smearing glue on the
teacher's chair. Some received their bottle like Long John
Silver getting the Black Spot in *Treasure Island*. The juke
box went dead, and the bumps and grinds on stage
stopped. I said just one short sentence, 'Seven fifteen
tomorrow morning in the chairman's office!' and they
knew I wasn't talking to the young lady on the stage who
was now buff to her tassels and G-string.

At seven o'clock next morning one of the sales team
approached me. 'I told my wife when you gave us the
thirty white Mustangs you were the most generous man I
ever met,' he said. 'Now I think you're the smartest, too.
Where can we hide a Mustang with five Indians on it?'

When the guys showed up at 7.15, I thundered just one sentence, 'Get the hell out of my office, and *for crissake* at least buy our beer.'

Of all the honours that were paid to me during my tenure at International Breweries, the most memorable was my adoption by the Indian Defense League of America. That happened in July 1964, about three months after my arrival in Buffalo. I was made a blood-brother and honorary chief of the Mohawk tribe. We actually cut and bled together. (For all concerned, I sure hope they're doing things differently in the AIDS era.) They gave me an Indian name *Ra-on-kwe-da-tsa-ni* — Man of Action. (Some of the Mohawks said it would better have been translated 'Man-who-can't-sit-still' and I couldn't agree more.) Surprising to me at the time, the women put the entire event together and did all the administration. A wise Indian woman took me aside and explained: 'You know who runs the Indian tribes? We do! Men *woo-woo-woo*, run around, and do the battle dance around the bonfire. The man makes the noise and goes to war, but the woman keeps it together. We make the traditions and tend to the future.'

'I see,' I said respectfully. 'Your people are more like us than I thought.' At that, she gave me a big hug.

But they aren't like us white folks. They're better. What generous people, the Native Americans! Back in 1849, when news of the Irish famine and Black '47 had spread throughout the world, the Choctaw Indians of Oklahoma, who were on the verge of starvation themselves, actually sent money to Ireland. What glee I feel now that the Native Americans are setting up gambling casinos all over the United States and raking in mountains of tax-free dollars. It will never make up for the way that we massacred their people and stole their land, but the gaming tables at least provide a bankroll for their future and their children.

The appalling campaign against the Native American was not a massive, well-orchestrated conspiracy. Instead, it was a series of small-scale, short-sighted, and individually rationalised decisions. Man never trips over mountains ... only over pebbles.

About eight months after my arrival, Iroquois Beer was able to recapture the loyalty of the buying public. We were making a profit even earlier. By September 1964, we actually made a profit in two consecutive months, something International Breweries hadn't done for the twenty-three previous months. We were shaking up the marketplace and attracting the attention of the mega-brewers. We were also attracting corporate raiders.

Steadily, the stock moved up from about $3 to $11. In large measure, it was because the business was slowly becoming more healthy and viable. Partly too, it was because investors recognised what we insiders knew. We were sitting on top of an asset-rich company. Investors, who were buying the stock under the street name of the brokerage houses, wanted seats on the board. I refused to buckle. Officers whom I thought were loyal to me disappointed me. The fight for control was long and complicated and ultimately hinged on a proxy struggle.

Under the headline 'Insurgents Win Brewer Control,' the *New York Times* described the dispute as a 'bitterly contested fight.' In the end, Dean Hawkland of the University of Buffalo Law School served as the chief election inspector. I still remember the newspaper photos of ballot boxes being carried by aides so they could be tallied. All the careful supervision made no difference to the outcome. I lost the proxy fight, but the new chairman asked me to stay on as president and chief operating officer.

Nope. I had other goals in my crosshairs.

With that, *Ra-on-kwe-da-tsa-ni*, adopted son of the Mohawks, bade farewell to frosty Buffalo and Tomahawk Brew with the *woo-woo-woo* beat out of me, but I had made plenty of *wampum* on the stock's steep climb.

What a lesson! My setbacks were becoming better textbooks for me than my triumphs. I figured if I could get this far with a business created by others, what could I do with my very own company? I had been reading in scientific journals and tinkering in my own garage. The time seemed ripe. You shut one door....

7

The Surge (1962–Present)

At the age of fifty, Al Roach decided it was time to create his own business, selling a product that had intrigued him for several years. On a visit to England in 1963, made after reading a technical article about how newly transistorised telephones needed faster-acting surge protectors (devices that protect lives and equipment from lightning strikes and other hazardous voltage surges), Al had an offer from an English company of exactly the technology needed. In 1964, he bought the rights for $60,000. Having left the brewery, he set up shop in his garage in 1965 and slowly added staff. By 1968, the company had moved from assembling to actual manufacturing at a plant in Farmingdale, New York.

Until 1984, AT&T and its equipment subsidiary, Western Electric, dominated the US phone industry. Although Al's product was superior, its initial market penetration hinged on approval by a key independent lab, the endorsement of a top regulatory agency, and the support of small phone companies, all of which happened between 1965 and 1972. But AT&T still refused to engage Al's company as a vendor of any significance.

In 1968, the company's stock was publicly traded. By 1971, it had moved from Farmingdale to Copiague, New York and employed fifty-five workers, with annual revenues of nearly $1.3 million. Faced with increased manufacturing costs, production was moved to the Caribbean in 1974. In 1980, frustrated that AT&T continued to ignore the company (now called TII) as a product source, the firm threatened to sue AT&T. In an out-of-court settlement, AT&T concurred with a $125-million 10-year purchase agreement. This milestone positioned TII as a major telephone equipment supplier. Since the break-up of AT&T, its successors account for about 85 per cent of TII's business today. With sales of over $50 million in 1997, TII estimates it has done well over $600 million in business since its inception. Al remains its chairman.

'How about taking a drive and having a picnic on Sunday?' Those could have been the last words before an ominous click ended a phone call between 'a young man and woman who were talking on the telephone during a thunderstorm.' That's at least how I imagine the conversation could have taken place. The facts of the case are accounted by Jim Romlein, President of MIS Labs, in the highly respected but very unromantic trade journal *Cabling Installation and Maintenance* :

> The young man put one ear against the speaker of a radio while the other ear remained pressed to the telephone. The young woman heard a sharp click on the phone and asked her friend about it but received no reply. The young man was found dead with one ear still against the radio and the other to the telephone.
>
> The click was the sound made by an electrical transient as it traveled down the telephone line. The transient, also known as a 'spike', resulted from lightning either hitting an aerial cable or striking near one. The high voltage traveled down the cable until it found a place where it could jump to ground.

'You're more likely to be hit by lightning, than to lose money on this real-estate investment' or 'He's as certain to go through with his marriage to Myrtle as he is to be hit by lightning'. Joking comparisons that portray lightning as an obscure risk are rampant. Unfortunately, the true facts are not so well known. In the United States alone, people killed by direct lightning strikes number about sixty to seventy each year, and lightning causes more than 26,000 fires annually, with a property damage toll of $2 billion. Ninety million bolts of lightning hit the US alone each year. In any electrical storm, 2 per cent of power and phone lines will be snapped by lightning strikes.

> In an electrical storm, a phone line is a lightning rod — an unprotected phone line is a direct-dial connection to death.

With the proliferation of personal computers and other electronics like high-definition televisions and audio and video CD players, the property toll will doubtless climb. While the fatalities might sound light compared with traffic accidents, they are horrendous when compared to other natural disasters. Over 51 years, the US National Weather Service has recorded far more deaths from lightning than from tornadoes, floods or hurricanes. These natural disasters draw media coverage because the scenes are dramatic and the rescue efforts immense. Lightning fatalities happen in isolated cases, but unlike many other deaths from natural catastrophes, they are preventable.

Manners and Mouthpieces I

At a critical business negotiation in Manhattan, the parties involved had to resolve a company merger fast, so all eight of us agreed that any phone call one of us would take would be fined $100. Twenty minutes into the meeting, a junior partner appeared at the door, nodded toward a prestigious Wall Street lawyer, and said grimly, 'Sir, this one, I'd take.'

Mr Barrister left. He slipped back into his chair 90 seconds later, dropped two $50 bills in the candy dish, and muttered, 'The little lady wants me to bring home a can of cat food.'

My first fascination with telecommunications was awakened during my time with Edwards & Hanly. I was introduced to an early manufacturer of internal telephone systems (PBXs or Private Branch Exchanges) who, back in the 1950s, installed their product in some influential New York firms such as Macy's and the *New York Times*.

Doing research on the firm, I developed a reasonable layman's understanding of telephones. When they discussed the installation of one of these phone systems, the engineers were talking about putting in 'protection'. I genuinely thought they were talking about armed guards. What they meant, it turned out, was a component with a chunk of carbon that would intercept and ground a big surge of current if it hit the phone line.* The carbon protectors had to be replaced when a surge passed through them, and the phones would be out of order until they were.

My knowledge about phones was helped by one of my brothers-in-law, who worked for the New York Telephone Company and could answer my questions. The engineers on the job taught me a lot too. I remember asking one of the technical people how serious this matter of protection really was, and he said, '*Deadly* serious — a lightning-induced power surge during a telephone call could kill you, if the line is not properly protected and grounded.' He pointed out a warning to me in the front of the thick city phone book (a warning you can still see in some phone books today) not to use the phone during an electrical storm.

---

* The late telecommunications industry historian Henry Altepeter estimated that Western Union's American Speaking Telephone Company operated 'some 56,000 telephones in 55 cities at the time it sold out to the Bell Co' in 1878. By 1900, he describes an array of protector devices that were being used including early carbon devices. (Henry Altepeter, *96 Years of Surge Protection*. A TII brochure.)

Manners and Mouthpieces II

Back in the 1950s, many fine Texas restaurants had a discreet sign at the entrance inviting gentlemen to deposit their six-shooters (which a surprising number still carried) before going in to dinner. Not long ago, I was at an exclusive Dallas club with a brilliant, but frail biophysicist sporting glasses as thick as binoculars. An Arnold Schwarzenegger-sized club manager came up to my friend and drawled, 'Park your sidepiece, Pardnah', meaning: CHECK YOUR CELLULAR PHONE. Today's club doesn't worry about someone shooting up the Tiffany glass. The problem is people shouting overseas over the foie gras.

As a fireman, I had seen my share of lightning-sparked fires. The realisation that lightning and the modern technology of telephones were somehow linked to create a hazard to human life intrigued and concerned me.

Furthering my education through the insurance and brokerage licences and attending Dale Carnegie had turned me into an avid reader of non-fiction. This was partly spurred by the research work on investments I did at the brokerage firm, but I also found myself drawn to technical journals. I was fascinated by the work of three scientists at Bell Labs — Bardeen, Brattain, and Shockley — who invented the transistor in 1947. I was an early investor in transistors. Not surprisingly, the first practical applications of the transistor were in telephones, although as *Newsweek* recently pointed out, Bell Labs didn't expect much of a payback from the transistor:

In 1952 Bell Labs offered to license the point-contact transistor for $25,000 against future royalties. They had few takers apart from a small Japanese start-up called Sony.[*]

No surprise that Sony has become one of the dominant firms that build consumer electronics.

Not long after learning about telephone-line protection, I picked up a scientific journal at an airport. In it, I found an article describing how the new transistor-supported phone equipment could not stand up to power surges on phone lines. The author predicted that there would be a need for a whole new line of surge protectors as those available couldn't fire fast enough to safeguard a transistor.

My first reaction was that of the former fireman, with an ingrained commitment to protect life and property. But this idea also registered with me as a former insurance broker. Thumbing through my actuarial tables to see what the real dimensions of the risk were, I roughly estimated the enormous potential costs. The fire in my belly was stoked as an entrepreneur and as an investor: some sort of technical solution *might* exist to respond to the challenge. Not being an engineer, I didn't have the slightest idea how to invent an answer in a lab. But as a street-smart kid from Harlem I had a hunch I could spot an answer if one smacked me in the face.

About six months later, I took a trip to England, where I had heard several companies might have a technology that could be close to the answer I was looking for. My visit brought me to a firm called M-O Valve, a subsidiary of the English Electric Valve Company. An engineer there asked me, in an almost offhand manner, 'By the way, would you be interested in a very fast-firing surge protector?' Mother of God, my smack had arrived!

---

[*] Begley, Sharon, 'The Transistor', *Newsweek Special Issue*, Winter 1997–98, pp. 25–6.

I couldn't believe my ears. Britain and other Commonwealth nations had been using this technology long before
transistors, simply because fast-firing surge protectors —
using a vacuum-sealed tube of rare gasses — required far
less maintenance.* The scientific journal article said that
this was just what the American market needed. I negotiated an option to purchase rights to the product for cash.
How much would it cost? They saw the potential for only
$500,000 in lifetime sales for the product, so they asked
$50,000 on the first day of our discussions. I came back
the next day and they had upped the price to $60,000. I
turned them down, but I left the door open a crack.

When I went back home, I studied the hell out of the
deal. These protectors were faster, but would they be fast
enough to handle transistors? Yes, they would. My con-
servative estimate was that there would be $10 million in
potential sales for that gas tube. Was I ever *wrong!*†

Later I found out that two other American firms had
toyed with importing the British surge protectors to the
US but backed off because the product didn't have Underwriters' Laboratories (UL) certification in the US, and the
US companies didn't want to go through the hassle of
securing this evaluation themselves. UL certification with
its implicit support from the insurance industry would be
crucial to selling. Still, I had conviction that the technology was right, and this investment *could* pump dough like
a wildcat oil well. So, not long before I went off to begin
my adventure in Buffalo, I asked M-O Valve one question:
'If I buy the rights to license this rare gas protector, do I

---

*   In more recent times, long-life light bulbs were developed and have
had a greater acceptance in Europe, especially in commercial applications. Europeans don't think of disposable in the same way as
Americans do. Also, labour costs are higher in Europe.

†   I was wrong — 5,900 per cent short! And, happily it will get even
worse this year.

also get the rights to any future improvements?'

'Why not?' they said. So I shelled out $60,000 and bought the distribution licensing rights in 1964.

'Do you want the rights to any improvements we might make?' I asked.

'Oh, no. That's not necessary,' they answered.

During my stay at International Breweries, I had no idea what I would do with my new industrial possession, but I incorporated a home for my surge protector investment called AJR Electronics. This did not really become a serious focus for me until November 1965, just several months after I left the helm of Buffalo's International Breweries. AJR started out as a distributor and assembler for the British-made products until I could really establish how worthwhile it would be to make them myself. My intention was to sell these units at about $6.50 each to parts distributors, like Graybar, who supplied telephone companies.

Every business begins with a risk that leaves a sinking feeling in your belly. Treat that feeling with three remedies: Research, Conviction, and Work.

We were putting together the protectors in the garage at our Levittown home. Assembly required inserting the tubes in a housing and attaching the needed wiring. In the beginning, the gas tubes came to us pre-assembled. Only later did we manufacture them ourselves. These were tubes the size of your little finger, and this version replaced an Italian format about fourteen inches long that did the same job. (The early miniaturisation has been vastly improved upon since — many of today's protectors are not much bigger than a pea. Others are about the size of a small appliance fuse.) Why didn't we bring in the protectors fully encapsulated and completely assembled? If we did, we'd be subject to an enormous duty. As it was, there was little or no tax on the component parts. The British manufacturer made the components to our US specifications.

At first, my wife and kids were involved in the business. The older kids helped with the packing and boxing of the orders — when we managed to keep them from horsing around in the improvised workshop. Dorothy — whose challenge of *if you're so smart, why don't you find a company and run it yourself?* had encouraged me first to take on International Breweries and then to start our own business — was a source of enormous support to me. She did the early accounting work, but we both still chuckle today at the number of items that ended up booked as 'Miscellaneous'.

I hired my first employee in 1963, when I was still working out of my garage. He was an engineer named Oley Wanaselja who lived across the street. Oley was a value engineer* in a big company that had down-sized. He was a good engineer and the first president of the company. Charlie Roberts was the second employee. He was a product-design engineer who really knew how to strip away what engineers term 'gingerbread' — embellishments that add cost but no utility. He had a sharp eye (I mean that literally, as he had tragically lost an eye in an industrial accident as a young man) for fundamentals and hated the word 'pretty'. What an engineer!

The order size grew from individual units, to tens, to hundreds, to thousands, and then tens of thousands. Gradually we were talking about a business of real size. After three years I saw that there was a market and bought the rights to manufacture the surge protectors in

---

* A value engineer evaluates production to improve quality, increase productivity, and reduce cost.

the US. That meant a small assembly plant and a warehouse. Those rights cost me an additional £50,000.

Although some lightning bolts are known to have the clout of a billion volts, smaller amounts of electricity, representing part of a strike, can be quite lethal. In a two- to four-mile radius of wherever lightning strikes, the voltage in any kind of copper is increased. And copper remains the heart of wiring. Both gas-tube protectors and carbon protectors are built to take surges of up to 6,000 volts. The difference is that a carbon protector can take such a surge only once, and must then be replaced or the phone connection will be broken. A gas-tube protector can swallow 5,000 such surges without deterioration. Assuming a hundred and fifty such surges a year, a gas-tube protector could have an average life of thirty years.

In those days, carbon protectors themselves cost about 25 cents and a unit assembled in its housing was roughly $2.25. The gas-tube protectors cost $1 and the assembled unit $6.50, including a fail-safe feature that blocked the flow of current, should electric lines collide with phone lines, as often happens in a storm. How could the gas-tube protectors possibly be cost justified?

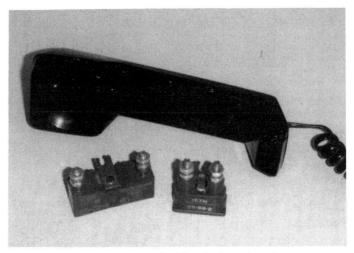

Surge protectors beside telephone handset

The answer was simple and powerful, but I had to go to Sweden to learn it. I visited the prestigious Swedish electronics firm L.M. Ericsson, and its head of purchasing asked the group how he could justify spending six-fifty for a surge protector on a telephone that cost only eight dollars.

His chief engineer — one smart cookie — was looking on and muscled into the conversation saying, 'Just, a moment! How much do we pay to send out a craftsman with a truck? Forty dollars at least or I'm Jiminy Cricket. And the government in Stockholm is yelling at us. The people without phone service are yelling at us, too. Roach's protector could last for at least twenty years. It takes the surges and grounds them, one after another, thousands of times.'

That session gave me the powerful selling point I needed to take back to America, and I did. We could save companies huge unnecessary expenses in service costs, and that began to open some eyes.

Initially, AT&T and the Bell System didn't want to buy components from a pip-squeak company like mine. The first challenge was to prove the superiority of the gas-tube surge protector. Trained in the insurance business, I knew the importance of a certification from Underwriters' Laboratories. Getting UL certification required sound communication and persistence, but it paid off.

Another very valuable forum for us stemmed from a socioeconomic trend underway. Telephone service was being expanded to the outback of America. Private enterprise alone could never have extended the telephone system to rural America — the wheatfields of Nebraska, the Florida swamps, and the timberland of Montana. The Rural Electrification Administration (REA), a US government organisation, subsidised utilities to get electricity to farmers and to have phones installed. This created a partnership between independent companies that were not part of the Bell System, and the REA. The big regulated utility had no interest in this kind of small-potatoes work. Who would want to stretch four miles of line to a farmhouse so that you could charge some cotton grower 80 cents a month for phone service? It could take centuries to recover the cost of the line! The REA loaned phone companies millions at 2 per cent interest for twenty years to bring rural America into the system. The net result was an enormous increase in the value of the American infrastructure. Through linking metropolitan and rural America, it created the greatest phone system in the world. These fledgling phone companies were especially sensitive to replacement costs. Also, the distances that ground crews had to travel to fix a surge protector were vast compared with repair service in densely populated urban areas. When the REA Telephone Standards Department — a demanding review authority — first approved one of our gas-tube protectors in 1965, that was a second important breakthrough.

Tampa, Florida is known in the telephone business as the lightning capital of the United States. Anyone who has ever looked out over Tampa Bay from a hotel room on a muggy September afternoon, will probably have witnessed Nature's greatest light-show short of the *Aurora Borealis*. Dazzling bolts of lightning dance across the Florida sky and punctuate the awesome rumble of thunder with hammerstrokes. Towards the end of the 1960s, we persuaded GTE, a leading independent telephone company, to conduct a major field test of our protectors in Tampa and the surrounding communities. We put a thousand of the new surge protectors side-by-side against a thousand of the old carbon units, and we waited for the bruising electrical storms to do their work. When the test results came in, we were victorious: our protectors reduced surge-induced maintenance and repair expenses in a range of 90 to 97 per cent over the carbon competitors!*

Armed with UL certification, REA Standards approval, and the Tampa Test, we had the ammunition to go after Goliath: AT&T. Until 1984, the vast majority of the US telephone business — equipment and service, local and long distance — was controlled by a single regulated monopoly: American Telephone and Telegraph. Its subsidiary Western Electric (and its associated research arm, Bell Laboratories) was the equipment expert. The regional phone company subsidiaries — the Baby Bells — handled local phone calls, and AT&T (known as Ma Bell) minded the long-distance business. It was one of the most powerful companies in the world.

Our relationship with AT&T — a small company doing business with a giant — merits close study by budding entrepreneurs with wares to sell to big business.

Even after the success of our 1971–2 tests with GTE in Tampa, AT&T refused to engage us as a vendor of any substance. By 1980, our frustration was kinetic. We had the products and the quality, but AT&T insisted on ignoring us, and we contended they wouldn't let us sell our products because they wanted their own subsidiary to sell the products instead to AT&T and its operating companies.

LeBoeuf, Lamb had just finished representing ITT in a case against AT&T that decreed AT&T had to purchase $300 million of telephone equipment from ITT. LeBoeuf,

---

* The Tampa test helped us with the general acceptance of the gas-tube surge protector. Since that time, we customise our products to particular needs. Protectors in hot, humid, and storm-prone areas like the US Southeast must match particularly heavy-duty specifications. Some urban areas need protectors with rugged housings to combat vandalism. Trends change too. For example, the late 1990s global warming pattern dubbed *El Niño* is said to have caused a huge jump in lightning strikes during normally frigid February 1998 in places like Long Island.

Lamb believed we had a comparable case, but they thought my suggestion of starting off the campaign with a letter was a good one.

David Overwhelms Goliath This Way

Small companies must take special measures to compete effectively:

- When one of your employees asks to do something in their off hours with a little seedling money, say yes. A brilliant Pakistani engineer Nisar Chaudhry — working in our laboratory after hours — produced one of the more exciting protectors in our arsenal.

- People in a little company stay where they are for years. In a big company they seem to change jobs every month. Make sure you stay on top of personnel changes in the client company better than they do.

- Always be ready to help when the customer needs it. However, present your case clearly if you believe clients are overstepping their bounds.

- Write contracts carefully regarding what you will deliver and when.

- When dealing with big organisations, always get your message to the top, not to the people buried at the bottom of the bureaucracy.

- Never forget you are fighting to survive and Goliath is hoping to continue to exist. The drives are different.

The lawyer's letter said that we believed our complaint was valid but we would rather have a business solution than a lawsuit. It was the only letter sent before our complaint was settled. After that, AT&T called up and said that they also would prefer a business solution. They wanted to sit down and talk about how to handle the matter. My son Tim, newly graduated from the 1977 Advanced Management Programme at Harvard, settled the matter at the Harvard Business Club in New York. He negotiated with Dr Bill Sharwell. Bill is a remarkable man with a keen mind. Later, he went on to become a loyal and trusted friend. At the time, he was a senior vice-president of AT&T. Some years later, after his retirement he became President and CEO of Pace University. A distinguished manager and author, Bill joined TII's board in 1995 and today sits on the boards of both TII and ABS.

Trust and Anti-Trust

- Competition is the essence of opportunity.

- The merits of the US Justice Department suit against software giant Microsoft have yet to be resolved, but the real issue in this litigation is one of opportunity.

- Preventing a competitor from 'doing it a different way' should never be the basis of restricting competition.

- Be prepared for the long haul. Often, a large company will contest issues where they have no factual basis and do so with the expectation that their smaller contestant will just give up.

- Entrepreneurs everywhere should be able to trust the law will support their rights to make the next breakthrough.

A major help in resolving the matter were our behind-the-scene connections in Washington. At that time Congressman Jack Wydler, a telecommunications expert and a good intermediary, was a pivotal player. The claim was settled in 1981. On 16 February, a contract was signed to buy $125 million worth of product sales over ten years. With the agreement's various clauses and other considerations, the value of the contract ultimately ballooned to $140 million.

When the government announced its plans to bust up AT&T in 1981 (the final decree to bludgeon AT&T was announced in 1982 and became effective in 1984), it really got my dander up, even though I was 67 at the time. Breaking up AT&T was the largest-scale regulatory action of the time and endangered the finest telephone system on earth. As part of the final efforts to avert the dismemberment, I testified before Federal Judge Harold Green in Washington that the dissolution of AT&T was a reckless step. I accused Washington of balkanising probably the finest industrial asset America had ever fostered, and blasted them for dismembering a national treasure. When the prosecutors accused me of testifying for AT&T because I had secured a big contract from them, I saw red. Indeed, although I respected AT&T's technological and business achievement, on two further occasions we were on the verges of major arbitration or legal action against them.

In early February 1982, the House Ways and Means Committee invited me to Washington to testify at the Hearings on private-sector trade policy, and I bemoaned the decision that had taken place. The week before I had purchased a full-page ad in the *New York Times,* which showed Uncle Sam lashed to the ground like Jonathan Swift's Gulliver while the Japanese marshalled their worldwide economic invasion. (At the time, the rise of Japanese economic might was the front-burner economic agenda in the US.) I used the occasion to assail the break-up of AT&T:

> Never would the Japanese Government have permitted the
> dismemberment of AT&T, the best communication system in
> the world; a company which took 100 years to build. A company,
> which, with its dedicated management and employees, and
> its technological contributions has contributed so much to
> the growth and greatness of America.

The thing that was making Japan so successful was exactly what AT&T had done. They had a complete infrastructure.

After the break-up, the Baby Bells weren't obliged to do any purchasing from TII. Between 1982 and 1987, most of the product AT&T was buying was being re-sold to their one-time Baby Bell offspring.

From February 1981 through 1987, AT&T lived up to all of their obligations to us, and they were a very good customer indeed — redistributing what we sold to them to members of the free-standing Baby Bells, as the dismemberment agreement permitted them to do.

Today, the Baby Bells represent a high percentage of our sales. We don't sell to AT&T any more — they would have no need for our products. In 1998, Bellcore — partitioned from Western Electric and Bell Labs and owned by the Baby Bells — sets the standard with a lot of help from innovative companies like TII. When we came out with a protector for the coaxial or 'cable' phone line, some say that Bellcore wrote their spec around our product. You can imagine the pride I felt when I heard that!

From a moonlighting entrepreneurial enterprise born in my garage, it's been an excursion. It took us thirty-two years to get to $50 million in revenues. Since we started, we estimate we have sold over $600-million worth of surge protectors; our core technology still remains gas-tube over-voltage protectors. We are the leading surge-protection supplier in the US. When phone companies tout 99.99 per cent reliability, it is largely because our surge protectors keep the lines stabilised and the connections up. Our strategy is built on three simple but sturdy legs, the protection of: life, property (including equipment) and profits. While our research and development and certain administrative departments are still located in New York, the company is now headquartered in Puerto Rico, and we are extremely pleased with our decision to base our manufacturing in the Caribbean. TII's stock is traded on the NASDAQ exchange, where so many of the leading technology equities are to be found. We got where we are because we have never forgotten who we work for.

Want to Get Richer?
Encourage Your Salespeople to
Earn More Than You Do!

- Don't cut a successful salesperson's territory unless they personally ask for help or smaller-scale work.

- Pay people for protecting and maintaining a contract, not just for getting new business.

- Reward team members for profitable sales, not just sales that add meaningless extra volume during a price war.

- Don't put a cap on bonus programmes because it looks like commissions are getting *out of hand*. I've seen companies with out-of-hand commission programmes that were rolling in dough, and plenty of firms with nice, neat bonus systems that were going down the tubes.

- *Make the people around you rich!* I'd never begrudge somebody for being richer than I am, especially if they made me ten times richer than I was along the way. Some salespeople at TII draw bigger pay-cheques than I do, and I wouldn't have it any other way.

How did we get to where we are? It wasn't because of some Harlem-born, Brooklyn-bred fireman. No sir! It was because of front-line tigers like Charlie Roberts, Frank Schleip, Dorothy Conboy, Al Dockweiler, Fran Giambanco in New York, and José Ramon Garcia and Greg Cortes in the Caribbean.

It was the likes of the late Henry Altepeter and a consulting lawyer by the name of Bill Sheehan, who had the horse sense to keep after me to buy the gas-tube rights after I got pissed off when the firm in England tried to jack the price up on me. After he left TII, Bill Sheehan went on to buy a fine stable in Kentucky and made a further fortune in harness-racing horses. Over dinner at London's Connaught Hotel one evening, I was feeling exuberant and predicted the stock would reach ten, before the splits and roller-coaster rides of the last decade.

Sceptic that he was, 'Never reach ten', was what Sheehan said, between the escargot starter, rosemaried lamb, and a bottle of Dom Perignon.

'Bet it does,' said I.

'Bet it doesn't,' said he.

On a napkin, with a Mont Blanc pen (back when a Mont Blanc pen was something special) I drew up a contract on fine Irish linen.

'Since this is an agreement between gentlemen, what do you want?' he asked.

'That 1971 ruby-red Mercedes convertible coupé we were looking at in the showroom window last week,' I said.

When the stock hit ten later that year, I was abroad on another business trip. The next morning I sent Bill a telegram:

==================**TELEGRAM**=================

(VIRGIN ISLANDS) BABY BORN stop WEIGHS IN AT TEN POUNDS stop EXPECT RED CARRIAGE stop REGARDS stop

===

When I got home, a brand new 1971 Mercedes 280 SL was in my driveway. Bill had lived up to the bet, that had also made him a wealthy man.

What does the future hold for TII? Not long ago, Bill Gates wrote in *The Road Ahead*:

> This is a wonderful time to be alive. There have never been so many opportunities to do things that were impossible before.*

I couldn't agree more, and I remember saying roughly the same thing to myself in 1935, in 1965, in 1995, and in all the years between! In a broader sense, Gates is right on. Our era — which probably began for me when I saw my first television set at the 1939 New York World's Fair — is one of the great eras in human history.

What has made this colossal change happen? Telecommunications breakthroughs have shrunk our world more than any force I know. Another visionary, Nicholas Negroponte of the Massachusetts Institute Technology (MIT) Media Laboratory, wrote in *Being Digital*: 'Distance means less and less in the digital world. In fact, an Internet user is utterly oblivious to it.'†

A phone cable that once brought us old Wanda, the nasal phone operator, whining, 'Number, *pleeze*' is now the link to televised rugby and soccer matches, on-line banking statements, Cyber-space pen-pals, and stock quotes. In the next century, at least 25 per cent of all work done will be done at home and sent off electronically to the office.

The consumers of electronic information are increasingly being stitched together by a fibre-optic web, but the facilities that feed that web are still vulnerable to power

---

* Gates, Bill with Nathan Myhrvold and Peter Rinearson, *The Road Ahead*, New York: Penguin Books, 1995, p. 276.

† Negroponte, Nicholas, *Being Digital*, London: Coronet/Hodder and Stoughton, 1995, p. 178.

surges, including lightning. Our Vice-President of Research and Development, Carl Meyerhoefer, predicts electronic and telecommunications protection will be a $2.2 billion market by 2001 in the US alone. According to a World Information Technologies, Inc., 1997 market study, the total US surge-protection market will grow at a rate of 12 per cent a year for the next four years.

How a Little Business Becomes a Big One

- Get experienced technical help early.
- Out-sourcing is popular today, but every time you put a component in the hands of a supplier, you amplify your own risk as to what you control.
- Never accept more new orders than you are sure you can deliver on time.
- You personally are never as important as your business. I dumped the name AJR Electronics along the way because my advisors told me it sounded like the name of the corner TV repair shack.
- Have customers stir the pudding. The more they feel the product is theirs, the less likely they will interfere with the order.

Fibre optic cable has huge information-handling capacity, but it is currently being deployed principally in the main telecommunications feeder trunk lines, and not at the customer's premises. It is not economically viable, at this time, to bring fibre optic cable directly to the home.

Moreover, converting optical signals to electrical signals in the home would be both extremely expensive and impractical, unless the optical signal could be connected directly to the end-user equipment (PCs, TVs, faxes, etc.) So, for the time being (a decade or more), the 'last mile' to the home will remain copper-twisted pair wiring or coaxial cables and, therefore, will require surge protection.

We talk about the delicate balance of nature — a fern on one hand and a rare bird species on another. In the electronic kingdom of your house, the same jungle laws prevail. Your grandchild flips on a hair drier in the bedroom, and an hour and a half of unsaved calculation crashes on the computer in the study.* We are learning that our new world has all kinds of risks associated with its dramatic new benefits, and TII is attempting to address those risks with new opportunities.

Phone companies install residential lines in housing developments now with two surge protectors rather than one. In the US, the one-telephone house is as obsolete as the one-car garage. That second line is certain to go somewhere — to the bedroom of the household teenager or into the fax or Internet connection for a personal computer or into a security monitoring device that keeps tabs on a holiday home. For TII, that means selling two surge protectors at least, where before we sold one.

Everything is going digital. Data is moving at a hundred megabytes per second. In minutes, you could dump the entire contents of the Library of Congress in Washington to St Kevin's Kitchen in Glendalough, if you wanted to. More and more, the premium is on surge protectors that do their job while distorting the signal the least.

---

* An effect of internal power line surge protection versus outside power line protection, but equally devastating, and something we are working on as well.

How big is the opportunity for us? We have thirty-six patents and not just in the telecommunications protection business but also in power protection, maintaining power during outages, and conditioners that stabilise the power supply and keep it clean. While surge protectors are not relevant to cell phones themselves, they are critical to the sending stations that allow all cell phones to receive signals. Since protectors of all sorts are more important to the integrity of data and safety of delicate equipment, we are lobbying the insurance industry to reward users of high-quality protection equipment the same way they cut premiums for customers with burglar alarms and fire extinguishers. You know those single plug-in surge *suppressors** that you plug into your personal computer or television set? One day, *smart homes* — wired for the state-of-the-art — will have a single *black box* that will integrate circuit breaker and surge protection for every plug input and every phone socket in your house. We intend to be the maker of that black box, because we intend to be the leading provider of protection solutions to the global market. And, I intend to be part of that surge as long as I can be.

---

* The distinction between suppressor and protector is important. A plug-in suppressor provides far less protection, and none at all if improperly grounded.

8

Another Table, Please (1970–Present)

As TII evolved, and especially since 1970, Al Roach has dedicated himself to two other initiatives. The first was the development of a strong public identity in speaking out on important issues. The second initiative, which has at times intermeshed with the first, has been to advance the commercial opportunities offered by environmental challenges and breakthroughs in biotechnology.

With TII's relocation of manufacturing operations to the Caribbean, Al became a vocal national figure speaking out in print and in person on both business and social matters. In 1982, he personally paid for a full-page editorial open letter in the New York Times *assailing the erosion of America's position in the global economy. The editorial prefaced an appearance before a Congressional sub-committee on US economic competitiveness. In 1983, the highly respected US business journal* Forbes *profiled Al, at the age of 68, as an industrial up-and-comer.*

Recalling the misery he had witnessed in Africa during his Merchant Marine days in the 1930s, Al steered TII into the water purification and aqualogy businesses in 1969. Water purification plants were constructed, and fish-farming initiatives led to his appointment as Honorary Consul of the Republic of Senegal in 1977 and to a 'bridge-building' trip to the People's Republic of China in 1979. The water-purification business was ultimately sold. TII's evolving Caribbean operations have made TII an economic development model. Continuing health trials, including a 1985 cycling accident and a 1987 bout with prostate cancer (which coincided with Al's championing of American research into superconductivity), deepened Al's convictions that wellness would merit even higher personal priority ... and could also offer great potential business opportunities.

'Al, why are you getting excited?
This is just nature's way of levelling the population.'

In my business ventures, I have underwritten the work of
many brilliant scientific minds — including some who are
destined for Nobel Prizes. Not that long ago, one scientist
came to me to discuss grant money for a new proposal. We
got into a fiery debate over a devastating disease wreak-
ing misery throughout the Third World. The scholar noted
with almost cynical detachment that my passion was out
of place. This was just nature's way of keeping the population in check, he shrugged. Fortunately, his proposal
wasn't that convincing to the scientists who evaluated it
for me, because I had lost my appetite for giving his projects further funding. That kind of indifference about the
sufferings of human beings runs contrary to a different
burner in my belly, a fire for fairness and compassion.

It wasn't always that way. That seven-year-old staring
out the window of a cold-water flat in Harlem was a
greedy little kid: 'What's for dinner under that shiny
silver thing? Can I have some *now*?' I had a caring side to
me, but mostly I was concerned with *me* making it. That
changed, but only gradually.

While it took time for me to get a better handle on
generosity, tolerance came nearly as second nature to me.
Tolerance, I am now convinced, is the best breeding
ground for sharing in an open-handed way. I credit my
mother Nellie and the environment I grew up in in Harlem as the foundation. Our neighbourhood was a United
Nations of backgrounds: Germans, Italians, Jews, Croa-
tians, and Irish, of course. When I was about twenty, I
remember asking my mother where my taste for different
ethnic foods like Kosher and Italian came from. She said,
'It's natural. You used to nurse off the different women in
our apartment house. Remember Mrs Castaliagno downstairs. I would holler down to her "Maria, how you doin'?

I'm empty. You wanna take him?" Or, it would go the other way: "It's OK, send Tony up.'" This was the original rainbow coalition on a random food chain.

The Dominican nuns also helped teach me the grace of sharing, but they did it in an unusual way. They made a *bully fighter* out of me. Sr Florita had an eye for bullies who would intimidate other children and would draw me aside, point at the culprit and hiss, 'Alfred, go get him.'

For a day or two, I would study the target. If he was the pitcher on the ball team, I'd deliberately step into a pitch and then run up to the mound swinging my fists and nail him. (If I got in a fight on my own, on the other hand, the nuns would wail the hell out of me.)

Plastering the Bully in the Belly (for kids)

There's not an iota of difference between fighting a bully on the school playground, and a bully who wants to terrorise you in business by alienating your customers. In my early years in the surge-protector business, adversaries against emerging phone-equipment companies could drip slow-working acid on phone lines, over which concrete blocks were then poured. The concrete would set and in days the phone lines would fail. Of course, no one wanted to tear up the pavement to fix the problem. It was no different from some teenage tough who would shake down younger kids for the money their mother had given them to do the family shopping.

- *Bullies work by fear.* The more they sense fear on your part, the more they will attempt to abuse you.
- *Bullies hate fair fights in broad daylight.* They lurk in dark alleys and sidestreets, and they let those surroundings amplify the fear people feel.

Plastering the Bully in the Belly
(for adults)

- *Teach kids to confront bullies.* One of my own children learned to face up to bullies only after he saw that a parakeet wasn't afraid to defend the space in a cage from an intruding human finger, even though the human being was a hundred times larger than the bird. Submitting to bullies is an unnatural instinct, a blockage of our in-born urge to defend ourselves.

- *No bully works alone.* Bullies succeed because of the silent approval of the peer group that surrounds them. In tough negotiations with unreasonable regulators I have always focused on where bullies derive their false authority ... and then done what I could to overcome it.

My outlook on our obligations to fellow human beings started to mature when I hopped freights during the Great Depression and saw hopeless poverty and true starvation. At home, we were poor, but there was always a hearty kettle of ham or chicken soup bulging with potatoes and carrots steaming on the stove. There were clothes on my back, and a bed to sleep in — even if some pushy brother crowded my space ('Shove your kiester over, and get your gawddam foot out of my face!') Organising the Thanksgiving food collection for the football team helped make me a Man-of-Action on the hunger issue. But what I saw in the Merchant Marine during 1938–9 made everything earlier look strangely civilised by comparison.

I saw starving people swim through floating human waste in a reeking harbour so they could fight over the apple and potato peelings thrown over board from a rusty Merchant Marine scow. Meanwhile, women and children waited anxiously on the docks to see who would win. To these people, the ship's mess on our freighter would have looked like the Captain's Table on the Queen Mary. The harbour, on the Cape Verde peninsula, is a fine one and was fertile once. By then, it couldn't even support the crudest sea-life beneath its surface.

At night, I and some of the other hands would throw over good food like oranges and apples, knowing the Senegalese would dive into the water for it. The steward would blow a gasket over this. We used to tell him it was Garbage for Goodwill. When I was a kid, I was very proud of being an American, because Americans just seemed to be naturally generous. To me, sharing seemed like an obligation. Sometimes, when Stew was drunk, I would go into the hold and shovel out rice and beans and sneak handfuls to the Senegalese.

When I ran the unloading crew, I would give the locals a tip of 25 cents, which equalled a day's pay for them. I'm sure I did no more than many visitors did when they saw the appalling poverty. In town, I tipped, too, but often it made no difference. I had porter after porter scurry away from me in a hotel lobby to pick up the bags of some nervous Brit yelling out 'Boy! Boy!', as if the British still ruled the seas and everything that touched them although the French had been boss in Senegal since 1815. Less intimidated Africans in the hotels told me that many English or Dutch treated them terribly, and these thugs got a charge from hitting them with ebony clubs or pushing them off the streets.

Imperialism — including the American ilk — was everywhere. When we sailed past Goree Island, the German first mate told me how many slaves had been transported from the Island's shackles to the plantations of North America. Goree Island was the moral and historical opposite of the Ellis Island that had welcomed my forefathers to the US. That night, I felt I could hear the clank of the chains and the cries of bitterness and grief.

The abuses I'm talking about are not ancient history. Not long ago, I woke up to a television report and saw people in Albania waiting for the refuse trucks to unload at five in the morning so they could piece together enough for a loaf of bread and make it through the day.

 Why Sharing is the Best Business

- International hot-spots — like Bosnia, Haiti, and Lebanon — cost wealthy countries vast sums in aid and intervention.

- People who cannot eke out a living in their homeland will always migrate, legally or illegally, and the cheapest solution is to have them stay where they are and prosper there as best they can.

- In any international aid programme, the worst enemies are almost always faulty distribution systems and corrupt middle-men who commandeer donated supplies. It is better to force immediate help into the hands of the people than to rely on greedy, bloated bureaucracies.

- Long-term population control and short-term human suffering are two separate issues. One should never seek to achieve the former through magnifying or simply permitting the latter.

- Never describe sharing as charity. Make it a loan, a lend-lease or a sale at a very reasonable price. Remember you are giving dignity as much as rice or shovels or medical aid.

In the early 1970s TII was riding high, and I decided to diversify. My first venture into the technology businesses had been successful. Why not another? Frequently, I saw reports that the world's water supply was endangered. Having lived on a sea-coast all of my life, I could see that humanity's precious water resources — sea-water and drinking water — were being abused. Gradually, thanks first to a growing awareness fostered by my wife, I became conscious of how we attempted to purify water with such dangerous chemicals as chlorine, which is reputedly carcinogenic. The average individual's lifetime intake of water is about 16,000 gallons, but it wasn't until 1829 — when the British first used sand-filtering on the Thames — that anyone ever attempted to clean up used water.* Water purification fascinated me because, once again, it had to do with saving lives at a primary level. Among the most immediate triggers for my interest were the emerging reports of makers of baby formulas whose distributors were discouraging women from breastfeeding babies, and instead encouraging them to feed the babies formulas, which the women often mixed with foul water, which in turn often led to infant deaths.

Our water technicians came up with some good patents, using sonics to break up the bacteria and viruses in the water, and ozone to kill or inactivate these microbes. We called the process *Sonozone*. In May 1974, we opened the *Sonozone* Wastewater Treatment Plant at Indiantown, Florida. We built five plants — in Florida, Puerto Rico, Senegal, Notre Dame at South Bend (where the research facility was), and Collegeville, Minnesota. We also built a commercial plant for General Motors in Michigan to process plating waste.

I met Senegalese President Léopold Senghor in the mid-1970s in Washington, where I hosted a dinner for

---

* *Life Magazine*, special issue, 'The Millennium', Fall 1997, p. 80.

him. I remember him as being about ten years older than I was. Senghor was born in Senegal but studied in Paris and was among the first of his nation to earn an advanced degree on the Continent. He was a brilliant essayist and poet and the first native African member of the French Academy. This combination of literary personality, concern for human rights, and rôle as a statesman has been seen in more recent times in the person of Czech Václav Havel. Senghor had heard about my work in water purification and aquaculture, and Senegal was having huge trouble with stocks dying out in their fish farms.

We favoured having them set up shellfish farms with *Macrobrachium Rosenbergii*. These are hardy fresh water shrimp, not prone to the diseases that often strike saltwater shrimp. (We proposed this aquaculture technology for China as well as Senegal.) When the brood stock has been created, the farm can live isolated from the wild surroundings. The animals are bred in cylindrical rearing tanks. In 1977, in appreciation of my efforts, President Senghor appointed me Honorary Consul of the Republic of Senegal in the industrial development sector.

Senegal also bestowed another great gift on me — my first awareness of the curative powers of cayenne pepper, curative at least for me. Unlike Gambia and other surrounding countries, the incidence of cayenne pepper in the Senegalese diet is very high. As a result, Senegal has a very low incidence of colon cancer and digestive disease generally, compared with its neighbours.*

The various water initiatives also helped strengthen my ties with the University of Notre Dame. My son, AP, was in the doctoral programme in South Bend at the time. On a visit to the school, I got to know Dr Joseph C. Hogan, who headed the School of Engineering. Joe was

---

*   For more on cayenne, see the Appendix entitled 'Volcanoes'.

especially interested in disinfection and sewage process-
ing. He suggested we set up a pilot plant at Notre Dame,
and I agreed. It was supported by the engineering department as a showcase for *Sonozone*. Joe and I developed
a great friendship. When he retired from Notre Dame,
where he remains Dean Emeritus, he became an advisor
to Georgia Tech. To this day, he remains on the boards of
our two largest businesses, including TII.

My relationship with Joe Hogan helped me to get to
know Fr Theodore Hesburgh, Notre Dame's legendary
and brilliant president from 1952 to 1987. Once, when I
was feeling bitterly inferior about my spotty formal education, I said to him, 'Father, if *only* I had that college degree.'

He looked at me with a smile and said, 'Alfred, tell me,
how many engineers do you have working with you?'

I scratched my head for a minute and told him twenty-
four or twenty-five.

'How many PhDs do you have working with you?'

'Six,' I said.

'How many other degreed technical people?'

'I don't know — maybe twelve.'

'Alfred,' he said to me, 'so far, I'm up to forty people
with advanced degrees regarding you as a leader. What do
you mean you don't have degrees? You have a team of
forty degreed scholars working with you. Think how many
people who have a degree with no one working with
them? But you found a way to get forty to work with you!'
Not bad, I thought to myself, when I looked at it that way.
In fact, I felt a little like scarecrow Ray Bolger in the
Wizard of Oz when he got his diploma.

Things were happening for us as far away as Senegal and
as close to home as the Caribbean. We could collaborate with
the emerging economies of the Caribbean in a direct way by
actually moving manufacturing facilities there. This move,
the first step of which was a massive relocation to Puerto
Rico, was to have great bearing on the evolution of TII.

Lessons for
Budding Entrepreneurs

The mistakes I made in the water purification, water disinfection, and aquaculture businesses were almost a manual in how *not* to tread water. Ultimately I had to choose between the water and the telecommunications businesses, as I couldn't afford to grow both at once. Budding entrepreneurs should take heed of what I learned:

- *Water technologies were not a division of the telecommunications business.* Investors couldn't understand why I was in two very different lines of business.

- *We tried to do too many different things at once.* People become suspicious if you try to do both water purification and water disinfection, because they suspect you are trying to treat raw sewage into drinking water. Aquaculture and fish-farming complicated matters further.

- *We banked on what was morally right versus what was economically feasible.* When OPEC forced oil prices up to $30 a barrel and environmental regulators kept the fines for water pollution artificially low, there was no economic inducement to do the right thing.

- *We were 15–20 years ahead of the times.* Water purification and bottled water have become two of the great success stories of the past two decades. I am told that the Texas firm that bought our water technology businesses in 1978 is doing well, but I don't want to know the details. In real estate, location is key. In new business concepts, timing is key.

One requirement for opening new doors in your life is firmly closing the old ones. Trends, public affairs issues and timing can mean everything for an entrepreneur.

I first saw Puerto Rico during the 1930s while I was in the Merchant Marine. I was drawn to the island, but repelled by the fact that an impoverished Puerto Rican *jíbaro* made a dollar a day, chopping sugar cane or bananas sunrise to sunset, and if he went home sick at noon he got nothing. The people were both very religious and very hungry.

Now the shining economic star of the region, Puerto Rico was known back then as the poor house of the Caribbean — running neck and neck with places like Haiti and Panama. People were either very poor or very wealthy; there was no middle class at all.

What gentle people! The stereotype that so many Americans have of Puerto Ricans is tragically false — Puerto Ricans *do not* act like gang members out of *West Side Story* and carry switchblades. I have carried out my own survey — wearing a *guayabera* and looking every bit the *Don* — and would ask Puerto Rican working men to lend me their knife. After nearly forty years, I have yet to find one who carries a knife. Gentle, but brave, Puerto Rico has produced more per capita congressional Medal of Honor recipients than any locale of the US.

My son AP was quite a help in resolving where we should put our first Caribbean plant. The shortlist had three possible locations: Mexico, Haiti and Puerto Rico. We analysed our options and it was clear that neither Haiti nor Mexico had the desired level of political stability. Puerto Rico had the best educational credentials and wasn't embroiled in political turmoil. So we made Puerto Rico our base of operations and kept research and development activities in New York. We moved our manufacturing operations to the Caribbean, and initially to Puerto Rico, because labour costs in New York would have put us out of business. In February 1975, we opened a 23,500-square-foot plant in Toa Alta, Puerto Rico.

Discontented mainlanders complained about my

exporting hundreds of American jobs to Puerto Rico. I explained that I was creating 450 *new* American jobs in Puerto Rico — jobs that would otherwise go to a place like Malaysia, then paying manufacturing wages of 15 cents an hour! In 1976, Puerto Rico took out a full-page ad in the *Wall Street Journal* showcasing our decision to open a plant in Toa Alta. President Reagan, Vice-President Bush, and later President Bush were appreciative of the support, recognising that economic development in the Caribbean was the only sound decision in the long term. As I have often said, it's better to build a factory than a gunboat.

Greg Cortes, the original vice-president and general manager of Puerto Rico facilities, set up the plant in 1974. He came from the TV manufacturer who had been there before. How we found him was nothing short of kismet. My son Tim and I were down in Puerto Rico talking with Fomento, the government economic development agency, staffed with highly educated and very dedicated people and an organisation that gave us enormous help. They had an industrial site in mind for us. We had just finished walking around the building. Coming towards us I saw this muscular and compactly built guy with a jaw that promised tremendous determination. I asked him if he knew anything about the building, and he said that he had been the general manager. 'Hell, come on and give me a tour of the plant,' I said.

He did. He joined us the same day and tried to retire five years ago, but I insisted I needed him. He promised to stay on until my retirement, and he's been a consultant since, with a very influential voice on everything we do in the Caribbean. Greg — along with people like José Ramon Garcia, Bartolo Alcantara, and John Hyland — helped build the foundations of our business. We continue to bring in talent that will help us build the glowing future we expect. Many of these young people have earned or are pursuing advanced degrees, like Raquel

Eunices Muñoz, who heads our industrial engineering department in the Dominican Republic. She received her industrial engineering degree in Santo Domingo and is pursuing her MBA at the Universidad Central del Este. The Caribbean has undergone great change in the past three decades. By the 1980s, it was clear that the US needed a more sophisticated economic development policy in the Caribbean. Castro was still a force to be reckoned with and world Communism was still alive and active in trying to broaden its beachhead in the Caribbean. Puerto Rico was itself developing into a high-wage market. I met with Secretary of State George Shultz to determine how we could better fight Communism. In 1982, President Ronald Reagan proposed the Caribbean Basin Initiative to Congress, and I was an immediate and vocal supporter. I met with Vice-President Bush on the Initiative and in hearings on the programme testified in support of it. The Initiative permitted twenty Caribbean countries to export to the US the value-added products they produced, duty-free for a period of twelve years. The CBI recognised that different parts of the Caribbean were at different stages of economic development and incorporated a Twin Plant concept. By 1987, it allowed us to perform labour-intensive operations in Haiti and the Dominican Republic and to do the final precision assembly and testing in Puerto Rico.

The latter was essential. 'Loaded' labour costs (including overhead and fringe benefits) compared this way in 1986: New York, $45 an hour; Puerto Rico, $22 an hour, and Haiti, $2 an hour (because the basic wage at that time was 39 cents an hour).

We set up a 70,000-square-foot facility in Port au Prince that had three hundred workers doing labour-intensive work such as handling printed circuit boards and winding coils. Haiti has traditionally had the lowest income on a per capita basis of any nation in the Western Hemisphere. The ruthless dictator Papa Doc Duvalier died in 1971, and his son Baby Doc was ousted in 1986 — the same year that the US charged Haiti with human rights abuses. The government bounced around for several years from junta to junta. Jean-Bertrand Aristide was democratically elected in 1990, but a military junta again intervened and seized power from him in 1991. The continuing political turbulence was too much for us.

We got everything out but the wallpaper. A military escort brought our caravan of equipment- and parts-carrying trucks right into the Dominican Republic, which is the other part of the same island. We had to move the facility out of Haiti because of the embargo put up by the OAS and in order to protect our shareholders' interests. One of the big disappointments of my career was that we had to leave Haiti. At that time 40 per cent of our volume was being assembled there. We got out merely weeks before the whole thing caved in. The operations we conducted in Haiti are now relocated to the Dominican Republic, and the Puerto Rican–Dominican Republic duo has been an outstanding combination for us.

* * *

Business was booming, but I knew that neither I nor my brothers and sisters were getting any younger. During 1977, when I turned 62, my sister Annie was diagnosed with terminal cancer. I swore that Annie would not suffer a similar fate as her daughter Patsy, who had died in my arms for lack of the medication she desperately needed. I went to Europe and visited a physician my wife Dorothy had read about. This physician, who was dedicated to holistic medicine, prescribed laetrile for Annie and actually provided her with a regimen of the drug. Laetrile, which is made from apricot pits, is banned by the FDA. A doctor dispatched the laetrile to the US. Annie took the medication, and her health improved greatly. I remember visiting her at her home and preparing a number of natural vitamin drinks for her. The medication and the high vitamin dosage seemed to help, and she began to regain some of the huge amount of weight she had lost. The European doctor predicted the improvement but solemnly cautioned against a blood transfusion after Annie took the laetrile.*

Annie herself and those around her knew about the warning. In the midst of this trauma, I was called away on business. Unknown to me, a transfusion was insisted on. Annie relented and was dead three days later.

Annie's experience made me rethink how I was treating my own body, and I came back to the moderation principles of Luigi Cornaro, but this time with a greater interest in healthy supplements to my diet. I was recognising that an ageing body had a more difficult time storing and manufacturing all the beneficial ingredients it needs for a healthy life. In the same year, I was diagnosed in the States as probably having a malignant polyp in my larynx and was advised to have it removed. The doctor in Europe who had helped with the laetrile looked at my throat, re-ran the tests and found the diagnosis ridiculous. He was right. It was just an inflammation.†

Boast carefully about good health. I remember a 75-year-old guy bragging about his vigour to reporters. He praised holistic medicine and then added he had sex twice a week. His wife happened to be in the crowd and asked sharply, 'With *whom*, might I ask?'

---

* I am not against transfusions on principle and have received dozens of life-saving blood transfusions during my life.

† Never toy with a potential cancer. Brenda Hyland, the wife of TII executive John Hyland, believes that early detection at the marvellous Sloan-Kettering Institute enabled her not only to survive breast cancer, but also to avoid radical surgery.

As I have grown older, injury and illness haven't stopped for me, but I have learned to handle them better. (My personal attack plan for vigour and well-being is outlined in an Appendix to this book, entitled 'Volcanoes'.) In August 1985, I was hit by a car while cycling in Puerto Rico. I suffered lacerations to the head, arms, and knees and was hospitalised for eight days in San Pablo Hospital in Puerto Rico. They had to operate to put things right, before I was transferred to a New York hospital for five days. The recovery included six weeks on crutches.

In 1987, I started the year with a fractured jaw bone following a complicated extraction of an impacted tooth. I was black and blue from my jaw to my mid-chest. My trigeminal nerve was damaged, and the pain was unbearable. In desperation, I visited Dr Peter Teng, an acupuncturist in New York City, every other day. The relief was a godsend.

Following this bout of pain, I decided to visit the Pritikin Longevity Center in Santa Monica and checked in there on Monday, 16 February. During a routine physical examination, the doctor detected a swelling of the prostate and suggested I see a urologist. Upon returning to New York and consulting with my medical colleagues, I decided on Dr Pablo Morales, in practice at New York University Hospital (NYU). My first visit to him was on Friday, 6 March. The following Monday, I was admitted to NYU and had a cystoscopy* performed the next day. The results showed that the tissue was malignant. The doctor said to me, 'Roach, you have three choices. At your age, you can forget about it... [I nearly socked him — I intend to be around for a lot longer, and already ten problem-free

---

*   In this procedure, an instrument called a cystoscope is inserted through the penis, allowing the urologist to examine the interior of the prostate and bladder. Several cores of tissue from the prostate are then obtained for biopsy through a needle inserted into the rectum.

years have passed since the condition was spotted and fixed.] or, you can go the chemotherapy and radiation route; or we can operate.' I asked another doctor what he would do. 'If it were me or my father,' he said, 'I would operate and put the genie back in the bottle where he belongs.'

If I chose radiation, and the cancer recurred later, they really couldn't operate because of what the radiation would have done to the tissue.

I now knew I had cancer, and I was facing a serious operation, but some really exciting news was breaking at the same time. On 20 March, the *New York Times* published a report on a remarkable breakthrough in superconductivity, which the *Times* compared to the 'Woodstock'[*] of physics. I was particularly fascinated by the work of Dr C.W. Chu at the University of Houston. On the same day as I read the news in the *Times*, the *Wall Street Journal* reported that the Japanese were poised to take an unbeatable edge in commercialising the new discoveries:

> In Japan [for example] companies that already sell conventional superconducting wire to the U.S. have begun crash programs to commercialize the new discovery.[†]

I immediately took action. I respected the Japanese ingenuity and determination, but I feared their increasingly dominant role as an economic competitor and the damage it was causing to the US.

Even though I was seriously ill, I was scheduled to give a talk before the International Policy Forum meeting in Banff Springs, Alberta, Canada, on 27 and 28 March. I threw my prepared remarks into the wastepaper basket and decided to talk on superconductivity instead, proposing

---

[*] Gleick, James, 'Discoveries Bring a "Woodstock" for Physics', *New York Times*, 20 March 1987.

[†] Kreider Yoder, Stephen, 'Japan is Racing to Commercialize New Superconductors', *Wall Street Journal*, 20 March 1987.

a debenture-funded joint public–private initiative to launch a US effort. It was a short speech. It may have been the best single talk I have ever given. Paul Weyreich, an aide to President Reagan, was present, and after I spoke, he immediately approached me and asked if I would deliver the same talk in the White House. On Monday, 6 April, I and two staff aides — Vern Whitt and Ellena Byrne — reported to the Roosevelt Room at 1.30 p.m. to meet with Dr William R. Graham, the Science Advisor to President Reagan. The meeting went very well.

The following day, I was in Dr Morales's office to make arrangements for my prostatectomy surgery. On 1 May, I made the first of many visits to the New York University Hospital Blood Department to start the build-up of blood stores which would be needed following my surgery. After one such visit on 12 May at 12.30 p.m. I flew to Washington to meet with Senator Jesse Helms at the Dirksen Senate Office Building. (The previous week, *Newsday* had interviewed me and described me as 'a crusty electronics executive who has taken it upon himself to do missionary work on behalf of the super-conductor.'*) There I presented Senator Jesse Helms with my case for superconductivity. Senator Helms asked if I would see the White House Chief of Staff Howard Baker. Within hours, I was back at the White House. After my presentation, Howard Baker said, 'Jesse was right, you are *quite* a guy!'

The following day, I flew to Houston to meet with Dr Van Horn, the President of the University of Houston. I also met with Dr Roy Weinstein, the Dean of Natural Sciences and Mathematics, and Dr Glenn Aumann, Associate Vice-President of Research. I had a long meeting with Dr Chu and also met his wife, Mrs Mai Chu, an executive with a Houston bank and a very good businesswoman.

---

* Schreiber, Paul, 'A Supercrusader for Superconductors', *Newsday*, 4 May 1987.

My operation took place on Monday, 25 May. For an older person, things happen to the body more slowly. The procedure took five hours in the operating room and six in intensive care. Nine blood transfusions were required. One of the donors was James Lilley, an African American evangelical Baptist minister and a veteran of Korea — probably the best chauffeur/bodyguard I ever had. He has the same blood type as I do. I looked over at him from the trolley I was lying on, smiled and said, 'Well, James, I guess I gotta sit at the back of the bus now.'*

The day following the surgery, I pranced around the corridors hooked up to my catheter and urine bottle, much to the amazement of the medical staff. On Wednesday, 17 June I was discharged from NYU.

The commercial opportunities in superconductivity may come more slowly than people expected, but I feel that I played a genuine role in spurring the sense of momentum behind this cause. I'm glad I had a month to recuperate, before I was invited to attend The 'Federal Conference on Commercial Applications of Superconductivity'.† The conference took place in the Washington Hilton Hotel on Tuesday, 28 July, and Wednesday, 29 July. It was keynoted by President Reagan. I was especially proud that the President's speech echoed ideas and even some of the language of remarks I had made in the White House to Bill Graham and then to Howard Baker.

---

* Until the courageous work of Dr Martin Luther King and other civil rights advocates, African Americans were compelled to sit at the back of the bus and other public transportation in the American South.

† The first thing I did when I walked into the huge meeting room was to button-hole one of the conference organisers and point to a sign overhead that read 'Problems in Superconductivity'. 'Not very positive,' I commented. The official nodded. In an hour, a new banner had gone up, reading 'Opportunities in Superconductivity'. When I saw the official later, I beamed a big smile his way.

After the President's speech, two secret service men appeared near where I was sitting in the audience and
motioned for me to come over. They said the Boss wanted to
see me. 'You don't raise your hand until he raises his,' one
of them cautioned me. (This was the same hotel, outside
which Reagan had almost lost his life in an assassination
attempt in 1981.) In a conference room behind the ballroom
where he had given his speech, President Reagan took my
hand and thanked me on his own behalf and on behalf of
the American people for what I had done for superconductivity. It was an unforgettable moment for me.

 Hear Ye, Mr President

My superconductivity experience taught me some important
lessons about how to be heard in key forums such as the
White House:

- *Be there at the beginning.* You have to watch for trends
  just as they are unfolding and be willing to take a leadership role before all the details are known.

- *Be brief.* Partly, leaders listened to me, because I was
  able to get out all of the important information in less
  than fifteen minutes.

- *Be visible.* My authority with the White House stemmed
  partly from my visits beforehand in Houston and to Senator Helms to explain that I knew what I was talking about.

- *Be focused.* I could have stayed home and fretted about
  my pending cancer operation, something over which I
  would have no control. Instead I chose to get something
  done where I could make a difference.

Health trials such as the bike accident and the cancer experience have made me think of retirement, but the thought has never lasted more than a couple of weeks. Someone once said of me that I retire every night and think it over in the morning. Those who retire are obsessed with memories. That annoys me. I'm not a reminiscer. I don't like to look at photo albums. I want to know what will be happening in the next ten years, not what some dog-eared photo said we did at a picnic thirty years ago. When people turn seventy, they generally stop planning and start thinking: What's going to happen with my inheritance? How will I best influence my granddaughter's education? How will I be buried? That's not planning; it's just sweeping up the remains.

Maybe I'm a little more cautious. When I turned 77, I had eight dental implants, which the dentist said would each be good for fifty years. I wanted to make the dentist a deal and pay 2 per cent a year. He turned me down.

Our age's greatest tragedy is when we look at somebody and count their calendar age against them. I fight back. Like Luigi Cornaro, I have learned to keep young people around me to keep me growing — taking courses, reading books, trying new experiences. I've also insisted that the older people around me keep growing. I used to say that most of my friends my age were watching the grass grow in Florida. Now the truth is that most of my retired friends my age are six feet under, *helping* the grass grow.

Nothing gave me more confidence that I was unsuited to retirement than when *Forbes* magazine — known as 'The Capitalist Tool', and both an unabashed business advocate and a no-holds-barred critic of the companies it covers — decided to profile me in 1983. All the business press and media experts warned me to stay away, saying that *Forbes* was going to smear me and TII. The opposite happened. TII was given a much-coveted inclusion in

'The Up and Comers' section. I was photographed working out in a gym, belting what fighters call a 'body bag' and cutting a pretty healthy figure for a guy of 68 in a green jersey and white shorts. Author John A. Byrne described me as '...a plucky, self-made Irish-American.' And regarding the 29 per cent ownership position Dorothy and I held in the company, he wrote:

> For an ex-Army welterweight with no formal education in engineering who has made his share of mistakes, that's quite an accomplishment.*

Reading that, I vowed to keep on making my share of mistakes and more, certain it would take me even further.

I met the late Dr Jonas Salk at my first meeting of the World Academy of Arts and Sciences of which I am a fellow. This particular get-together took place in Minneapolis in September 1994. (This august body meets only once each five years.) For me, Jonas Salk was always the Julius Caesar of bio-medicine. He beat polio and, had he lived long enough, many thought he would have done the same to other infectious diseases. I was to turn 80 in a matter of months. Dr Salk already had about a year before. He recalled the book *Life Begins at Forty*, and we were both bemoaning that that truth had a certain pain when you were about to turn twice that age.

These people at the World Academy are shrewd. They put me on the roster to speak after Dr Salk and assigned me the topic of ageing. My reputation for looking at the positive side of things preceded me. I delivered my usual off-the-cuff talk, this time blending optimism and acceptance. I started by reminding people that Jonas Salk had extinguished the quiet dread of polio, especially in the summertime. After the Second World War, it was the real

---

* Byrne, John A. 'Up From Harlem', The Up & Comers, *Forbes*, 21 November 1983.

fear in the hearts of parents (look how it had stricken the mighty Franklin Roosevelt), keeping them and their families away from the local swimming pool.

Then I suggested that Dr Salk tackle the next most formidable problem, which was — flaunting my self-interest — ageing; and I, being no shrinking violet, offered to help set a framework. Ageing is a three-part problem, I asserted: it's chronological, biological, and psychological. You can't do much about chronology, because its etched in stone or penned in ink and it's all over the place. Biology, you can influence with what you feed yourself and how you treat your body. Psychology is up to you when you stare at the mirror every morning.

I told the group — which was one bunch of top people — that I probably had the most perfect time in my life when I was welterweight champion at 18. Chronological, biological, and psychological were all pumping together in one mean machine.

The Secretary General of the World Academy of Arts and Sciences, Dr John Proctor, who is also on the Advisory Board of American Biogenetic Sciences, the subject of the next chapter, would not let me off the hook. He asked: 'Alfred, aren't you forgetting about the *fourth factor*?'

'What could that be?' I asked.

When Dr Proctor intoned the word, 'sex-o-log-i-cal' the audience damn near busted their guts!

I paused for a moment, and then asked my cohorts, 'Fellow members, will you join me in a chorus of "Memories"?'

First we sighed, long and deep, and then we sang.

9

Brainpower (1983–Present)

In 1983, at the age of 68, Al Roach founded American Biogenetic Sciences (ABS). The business had no particular goal at its outset, although Al saw coronary and neurological ills as top priorities.

For the first six years, Al personally funded ABS's ventures and quickly discovered that biotechnology was a very expensive business and that it required time and effort to assemble the gifted specialists needed to do the complex work. In 1990, ABS was made a public company and since then has raised more than $50 million in market funds to finance its research. Through ABS, Al increased his contacts among the scientific community, and he sharpened his thinking on running a biotech business. ABS specified the mission as developing patentable diagnostic and therapeutic products in cardiovascular and later neurological medicine.

Watching modern scientists interact with each other through such means as the Internet, Al devised the idea of a Global Scientific Network in 1992. The Network positioned aspects of ABS's research (especially its neurological interests) as a 'virtual company' — linking distinguished scientists worldwide — and enabled the development and ownership of intellectual property without investment in costly laboratories. The Network's tentacles extend from its Dublin hub to other primary centres worldwide. In 1997, strategic alliances were also signed with the Russian Academy of Sciences and the Chinese Academy of Medical Sciences, which he believes may establish a platform for future research. Although its focus is on brainpower rather than elaborate facilities, ABS does operate a patented antigen-free mouse colony producing antibodies used in diagnostic products that can predict the formation of blood clots. To date in 1998, ABS has yet to show a profit, but it has begun to move from the pure research to the marketing stage in several of its products. Long lead-times are common in an industry where patiently spent years can be followed by huge breakthroughs and vast profit windfalls.

'Phone up your lovely wife, and tell her she's going to bed with a millionaire tonight,' I told the researcher solemnly.

'Just wait one damn minute, Roach,' the irate scientist shouted at me, his eyes flashing wildly. 'You wouldn't *dare* personally exploit our professional relationship and the funding you have provided for these studies. *You wouldn't dare...*' When he snapped the pencil in his hands, I — who have experienced a broken neck — winced at the crack.

'For the love of God,' I smiled, 'hold onto your horses! Have I ever asked for anything *remotely* like that before?'

'Well, no, but there's *always* a *first time*,' he hissed with bitter suspicion.

'Whom does your wife normally go to bed with?' I asked him, as I rested my arm around his shoulder.

'Well, with *me*, of course!' he bellowed, his face still white with anger.

'And so it shall be tonight,' I assured him. 'I'm not the only millionaire in town,' I continued. 'Tonight, your wife's partner will be the same, but your wife's partner's *wallet* will not. It just got a whole new facelift.'

Then I explained the effect of our most recent update. The benefit would be for our shareholders generally, but would also have a sizzling impact on his stock options and incentive payments — a big reward, but well deserved and fully in line with industry practices and the formal agreements. When it all soaked in, my friend didn't know whether to laugh with glee or cry with appreciation.

I love scientists ... and I just love to shock them, too. For all their analysis and systematic thinking, many are so easy to fool on matters of human nature. I couldn't resist breaking the news to this distinguished researcher in the way I did. Needless to say, he phoned his wife and pulled the same stunt on her. 'Al Roach just marched into my office and said, *in no uncertain terms*, that you will be going to bed with a millionaire tonight....' I could hear the gasp on the other end of the line.

Al Roach's Golden Rule

What's the smartest way to cast bread upon the waters?
Make as many millionaires in your deals as you can,
especially your stockholders and employees!

In 1983, at the age of 68, I founded American Biogenetic
Sciences (ABS). Water purification, initially developed in
a subsidiary of TII, was really my launching pad into
biotechnology. After we sold the water-related businesses,
my interest in advanced sciences continued, and I needed
a new company as a vehicle to launch an entirely fresh
strategy. This time I decided to make it a free-standing
business, totally separate from TII. I had no particular
project in mind, but several priorities spurred me to start
a company, and the initial drive may have been fuelled by
little Patsy dying in my arms when I was a fire warden
during the Second World War.

I was keen on investing in breakthrough work to combat heart disease, and, later, neurological diseases such as
Alzheimer's. There was also a self-interest element: I had
followed the stock market and seen how a brilliant research insight could have a terrific financial payback.
Personally, I'm partial to odds when they're a thousand to
one, *if* you assemble the right talent to overcome the odds.

As ABS evolved, several operating criteria became
clearer. The firm would focus on the invention of diagnostic and therapeutic* medical products and aim at
securing key patents for them. It would work without the
huge fixed costs of a major laboratory or research facility

---

* A diagnostic product (like a test for blood-sugar level) tells you if a
problem exists; a therapeutic (like insulin) treats the problem.

and have a tiny but high-powered central staff. It would gather the best scientific minds available around clear and specific targets, tapping only that portion of their professional work directly related to ABS's goals. It was only after ABS had been around for a decade that we created the mechanism that would fuel that kind of collaboration — the Global Scientific Network, a concept that must be understood in the context of my overall views on medicine.

Biotechnology marked a true change in traditional medical thinking, especially in strengthening people's own immune systems to cure their illnesses. Targeting medication in smaller doses, with more precise formulations, has also gained favour. The main benefit of targeting is that it goes to the site where it is effective, rather than all over the body in a random way. Medicine should go to the organs and tissue where it's useful and not to places where it causes undesirable side-effects. Miniaturised procedures — such as endoscopic surgery — are revolutionising how operations are done and drastically reducing the side-effects. I recently read that it will soon be possible for a surgeon in, let's say, Kansas to operate on a patient in Florida simply by having his or her hand motions transmitted by signals over phone lines to control instruments in the remote operating room.(Will those surgery phone lines ever require the best engineered and most reliable surge protectors, too!)

When I formed ABS, I was prepared to hang tough, but I never expected it could take a public company ten or more years to generate a profit, and scoffed at advisers who said it would take three or four years *minimum* for the company to prove itself financially. I figured I would spend $500,000 of my own money, and then I'd be in clover. My lawyer, the distinguished Leslie Misrock, shook his head, grinned, and warned that the half million would be gone before I knew it. He was right, but my faith longer term remains unshaken.

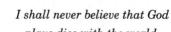

I shall never believe that God
plays dice with the world.

A. Einstein

If humanity never bet on a long shot,
we'd all still be living in caves.

A. Roach

Since ABS's Global Network started out and looked for good projects to fund, we have been bombarded with proposals. On the surface, most look like they have merit. But we are a relatively small company and our standards have increasingly become tougher.

To strengthen our focus, we keep pruning out the dead-wood and the weeds among our research portfolio. No matter how much we love a researcher as a person, we trim funding back or eliminate it entirely if the criteria aren't met.

For the first seven years, I supported ABS privately, out of my own wallet to the tune of $4.5 million. We went out on the road to build the business in 1990, having become a public company in May of that year. Since then, we have raised $56.5 million in public funding through our stock market offerings, and we feel a very clear accountability to our shareholders.

How does a biotechnology company produce something
that will bring rewards to its shareholders?

Many modern pharmaceutical breakthroughs were discovered and developed in biotech companies. These firms create substances that are proven effective in tackling disease. They must be approved for use by government regulators and used and recommended by doctors and hospitals. The US Food and Drug Administration has increasingly become the global norm for evaluating and approving drugs for sale and use. The FDA requires that a drug be shown to be effective and that it be largely nontoxic. The benefits have to outweigh the risks. It's also desirable to show the drug's 'mechanism of action' — how it works — and that can be as elusive as hell to describe.

Research: The Dough Recipe

Every biotechnology firm bakes its bread in a different way. We ask the following questions to decide whether a project meets our particular criteria for the research we'll fund:

- Is there a close fit between the idea and our chief research initiatives (i.e., cardiovascular medicine and neurobiology)?

- Is the idea patentable and/or does it lend itself to one of our existing patents? (There are countless interesting ideas to explore, and a limited stock of financial resources. We are a commercial firm and owe it to our stockholders to pursue those projects where we can secure a position.)

- Have the researchers proven the fundamental concept? Has the viability of the concept been shown in the laboratory or, better still, in the clinic?

- Does the project have clear milestones for measuring progress and do the researchers have a track record of being successful and systematic measured against research milestones in the past?

- Will the researchers be good, respected collaborators with others in our network?

It takes about seven to ten years to develop the average drug, with a typical investment of $150–$250 million and sometimes much more. The lion's share of the cost is in the later stages of drug development, those that involve advanced animal and human testing. ABS focuses on the *invention* or discovery of potential new drugs (we call them compounds), and we leave the expensive later development process to the huge pharmaceutical giants we hope to have as partners. Such firms are among our most important potential customers for buying licences to technology we own in various stages of development. Overnight, a promising compound can be licensed for tens (sometimes even hundreds) of millions of dollars, depending on the stage of development and the licensed indications.

Inventing or discovering a compound and bringing it through the first testing stages — our slice of the development path — often costs $10–12 million, and rarely less. Every time we bring a compound a further step along its development, we reduce the risk (both for companies that would license it and for doctors and patients who could end up using it) and add to its value. Each successive step — from the first simulations in a test tube — clears up a question. We leave it to the bigger companies to determine the safety, effectiveness and dosage for humans, but rigorous earlier testing is usually a good indicator.

Emer Leahy, ABS's Senior Vice-President of Business Development, was one of the youngest people ever to receive a PhD (in just over two years) in her discipline at University College Dublin. A gifted woman, she is steering the development process so we get the greatest possible value from the patents we own. She is also helping us to focus further development on those compounds that will give us the biggest payback. She's out forging strategic alliances and acquisitions of smaller companies, so our primary emphasis shifts from research to making products and ringing the cash register.

Once you have an actual product, the drug companies must still be persuaded it's worthwhile. That means getting a compound into leading research hospitals so that it can be 'field tested' and endorsed by top medical authorities. It can also mean explaining to regulators and insurance officials how a product can reduce costs and improve medical service.

When I started ABS, I realised how little could be done in one lab. There had to be a way to connect all these good scientists together. My mental model was the collaborators who worked together on the Manhattan Project that built the first atomic bomb. Why not put together a private network, built on the same principle and apply it to peaceful rather than military ends?

Instead of a multi-million dollar building, I wanted an electronically connected brain trust that could span the world, day and night, and defy the constraints of bricks and mortar. Rather than building facilities and putting people in them with 100 per cent dedication of their time, we have selected premium specialists in certain areas, and call upon them in very focused ways — rewarding their participation with stock options, earnings from patent and licence revenues, support for their research, consulting fees, and access to the leading scientists in their field or in the related disciplines they need to reach their goal.

We decided that what would make us unique would be a truly global network. So we selected various individuals (along with the locations where they were to be found) we thought would be the most promising for future technology research. The United States is the world leader in biotechnology. We knew we had to have a presence in the States. We chose Ireland in Europe, both because some of the titans in neuro-sciences were to be found there and because it was destined to become the most dynamic economy in the European Union. Look at the country's educational attainment compared to the rest of Western Europe — the level of college experience is more than twice the EU average.* In Europe, we set up collaboration agreements with scientists in places like Ireland, the UK and Germany, where we identified experts who were exactly matched to the problems we were addressing. Israel was a further goal for us, with the dramatic achievements in science and technology that country has made in record time. China and Russia became the remaining hubs because the pivotal geopolitical revolutions of the past two decades suddenly connected these two scientific powerhouses to the Free World and made vast reservoirs of people and know-how available to us.

Methodically, and especially through the work of Ellena Byrne, our Dublin-based Executive Vice President of the Global Scientific Network, we learned who the leading authorities were in those science areas we wanted to emphasise. In the five years between 1992 and 1997, the profile of the Network was forged.

We went directly to the researchers who developed the models in areas where we had an interest. We established relationships with people like Professor Rem Petrov, the distinguished vice-president of the Russian Academy of Sciences, and I have tapped into the intellectual resources of his team from time to time. Other biotechnology companies also comb the universities for technology, and they collaborate with academic institutions to develop some of their products. But they tend not to venture out as far as we do in seeking technologies in places like Russia, China, and Israel. ABS is unique, having become what we wanted it to be —

---

*   Sweeney, Paul, *The Celtic Tiger: Ireland's Economic Miracle Explained*, Dublin: Oak Tree Press, 1998, p. 104.

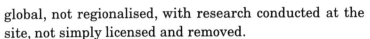

global, not regionalised, with research conducted at the site, not simply licensed and removed.

The Global Network was set up person-to-person and eyeball-to-eyeball, talking with players and engaging them directly. It took several trips to launch our initiative in Russia. On visits to Israel, we met with as many as twelve people separately in one day. Ellena and I were able to build the Global Network only with considerable help. ABS has local representatives who speak the language, and they organise logistic support services in the markets most distant from Ireland and the US. We have top-notch people in Russia (a great linguist), in China (our administrator is in charge of passport control), and in Israel (a PhD well known to her scientific peers).

The scientists are both the *producers for* and the *customers of* the network. Only three to five of the many labs in our network might be involved in the study of any one particular project. Yet, we do all we can to keep them alerted to opportunities, so no untapped synergy lies dormant. Motivating and energising the network is the particular value I try to add to ABS. When a scientist gets frustrated, I'll step in and suggest, 'Why don't you call so-and-so?' Part of my job is to remind people how sizeable and rich our network is. My second chief role is to help scientists respond to both business opportunities and threats. My grasp of the commercial potential in a product is pretty quick. More than once, I have taken an overnight flight out of Kennedy over to London and hopped a connecting flight to Dublin to pre-empt valuable research rights being sucked up by competitors.

What exactly is it we are in the business of developing and selling?

For the $56.5 million of public funds invested, we have stitched together some formidable clout and impressive intellectual property.

Our first big asset, after our scientific talent, was our
mouse colony. These mice are absolutely antigen-free:
They don't have antibodies to bacteria and viruses, because they have never been exposed to the contaminants
that cause them. As a result, it is possible to produce
monoclonal antibodies that you can't generate in conven-
tional ways. Each of these antibodies is a molecule that
detects a foreign particle such as a pathogen — a bacteria
or virus. The therapeutic and diagnostic benefits of such
antibodies can be enormous.

It took years to develop the mouse colony and to work
out their special food — a liquid diet of amino acids. Over
time, we have made major advances in the quality of the
diet. We manufacture our own food. One litre of our
mouse food would weigh 10kg (more than 20lb). A litre of
water by comparison weighs 1kg (a little over 2lb).

Jim McLinden is originally from Kansas where he
raised cattle. His PhD, from the University of Kansas
Medical Center, is in microbiology, with an emphasis on
protein purification and bacteriology. His post-doctoral
training was in molecular biology at Ohio State University. One of the most loyal and dedicated professionals we
have in any of our companies, he has been known to roll a
cot into a lab so he could monitor a test every two hours
over a three-day period. With all his brains, Jim's drawl
and manner bring to mind a prairie cattle boss.

'What's the big difference between breeding cattle and
breeding mice?' I asked Jim once.

He scratched his jaw as he thought for a second. 'Well,
ya know, mice are a lot smaller and eat a lot less ... and,
the work for the ranch hands tending them is a lot
warmer. But the principle is the same.' Romance is romance, I guess.

We maintain a colony of 140 mice — 60 to 70 are
breeders, 30 are adolescents, and 30 are pups. Jim has
been trail boss (director of the laboratory) for the colony,

for about four years. He has been at ABS and worked with mice for eleven years.

Not long ago, we moved the mouse colony to a site several hundred miles away. This required careful planning, which Jim and his colleagues did like true pros. We put the mice in sterilised containers; they were on battery-powered air suppliers with a continually filtered flow of air, and didn't even know they were leaving home. The move was made at a weekend. The supporting trucks were lined up in a caravan as though for an invasion. We loaded the animals onto a van and set off on the eighteen-hour trip. A new isolator* awaited the mice at our destination. As the mice had be fed regularly or they could die, we would stop each six hours and break out the food — not unlike taking the family to McDonald's on a long trip. We had no casualties. After the move, we *did* have a thirty-day period of slowdown in breeding, but such a lacklustre interest in the opposite sex is routine in the coldest part of the winter. (Why do you think Valentine's Day is celebrated in the middle of February?) We turned the lights lower (really!) Next time, we might try a little mood music in the background.†

Many people who are overweight and over sixty exercise little, suffer from high blood pressure, and have a family history of coronary disease. In short, they are in the high-risk category for a heart attack. At about five or six in the morning (when most heart attacks occur), they might wake up with moderate chest pains and some shortness in breath. The situation gets their attention, but it doesn't seem compelling enough to have them call

---

* An isolator is the completely enclosed and sterilised housing unit in which the mouse colony resides.

† I can assure you that in our laboratories, no animal has ever been sacrificed needlessly or suffered unnecessarily.

their doctor or go to the hospital casualty department. How much would those people like the peace of mind offered by a kit in their medicine chest — a kit that would let them prick their finger and determine in minutes if a dangerous blood clot was forming in their system? In the coming years, such a kit might be as commonplace as a home pregnancy test or the test diabetics use to monitor their blood sugar. This innovation has been one of the most promising by-products of our beloved mouse colony.

There are many irrational fears about biotechnology research. There is also a lot of human suffering that could be averted if more people supported it actively. I have long admired what Bertrand Russell said about fear:

'Fear is the main source of superstition, and one of the main sources of cruelty. To conquer fear is the beginning of wisdom.'

Impatient for more tangible results, I gave our cardiovascular scientists a challenge several years ago. It was to focus their work on one tangible result. 'Give me a niche,' I pleaded, '— a single niche, where we can do something interesting.' Eureka: our mouse colony cells produced antibodies to detect the onset of blood clots. In fact, these antibodies which identify a marker in blood, give us an early warning that something is happening — a heart attack, a stroke, or deep-vein thrombosis.* The earlier a problem can be detected, the more successful the treatment.

---

* A thrombus is the medical term for a blood clot.

As a result, we already have three diagnostic products in this area. Two have been cleared for marketing by the FDA. The first, called TpP, is a test for the risk assessment of blood clot formation. The second, FiF, assesses the risk of coronary heart disease. Both are designed for hospital testing now. A home version of either of them is still a matter for future speculation. Our third product is an imaging agent that can be injected into a person. Not only does this diagnostic product visualise the clot, but it also directs therapeutics to the site of a clot problem — much as the guidance system on a Patriot missile hones in on a target — helping to break up the clot. To give an idea of the market sizes involved, we are talking about the potential for coronary heart disease tests numbering 350 million a year.

In the neurobiology area, we are even more virtual than in the cardiovascular business. No mouse colony, just the best human brains in the business, systematically plotting how to attack those awful degenerative illnesses, like Alzheimer's Disease and Parkinson's Disease, which affect the human brain. We have some remarkable patents and are developing some exciting products.

Scientists used to think that the brain had 100 million neurons. Now, the number normally discussed is in the tens of billions — equivalent to the number of stars in our galaxy, the Milky Way. Each neural connection underpins a memory, a thought process, or a body function. We study those connections closely and have a special interest in compounds that help animals retain learned behaviours even as they age or their brains are damaged.

Our neurobiology researchers are probing four key conditions: Alzheimer's Disease, Parkinson's Disease, stroke and epilepsy. In all cases, we are interested in drugs that protect neurons and have fewer side-effects than currently available substances.

Names are More than Games

I am a firm believer in leaving things up to the scientists and the mice, with few exceptions. One of those exceptions is the name that we stick on the product before we sell it.

After a bottle of wine one evening, I asked what our product was going to be called. My associates said they'd like to name it after the initials of a colleague who had died tragically. Not a very encouraging idea to someone who's afraid they're going to die of a heart attack.

'How exactly does this diagnostic function?' I asked.

'Well, it's a *thrombosis precursor protein*.'

'Now, we're on to something,' I said as I ordered our group a second bottle of Medoc. 'Isn't there a very highly regarded therapeutic drug called TPA also used in the treatment of coronary problems? Why don't we call it TpP?'

And the diagnostic test was so baptised.

I had previously learned when I renamed AJR Electronics as TII that a solid, easy-to-remember name can be a definite marketing advantage. That's especially important for pharmaceuticals. When doctors are under a lot of stress, an easy-to-remember name helps.

Just before Christmas 1997, ABS researchers brought me to a laboratory at University College Dublin. They sat me down in front of a personal computer, and I flipped through a presentation on compounds that were slowing down deterioration in memory connections. Time after time, I interrupted the presentation and asked for an explanation in unadorned Brooklynese, and they patiently translated their findings into lingo I could handle. Then I observed a rat* — in his golden years, as they say, but injected with one of our compounds — swimming towards a submerged platform in a tank filled with warm water. (Every morning that I struggle out of bed and into my jet-stream pool, my sympathy for that old rat grows.) Our researchers know how fast a normal rat can learn this behaviour, and they know the age factor — how much slower it is for an old rat to learn the same thing.

The next swimmer in on the starting line† was a younger rat, trying for the same goal. He may have had a sleeker tail, but the young dude didn't have the same fire in his belly as his predecessor. Sure enough, when they punched the stopwatch, the aging geezer had won the race. I cheered my lungs out. Further proof that old age and treachery will always win out over youth and skill!

What all this means for humans, we have yet to see, and I hope I'm around to see it. When I watched the freestyle swimming match — just one of thousands upon thousands of such experiments performed within our Network — and reflected on the future of the youngsters in the Christmas carol concert I had just attended at St Paul's school, I thought that this is indeed a wonderful and somewhat zany time we live in. I hope that those children will look back someday and say that their parents and grandparents truly left them a legacy of discovery on which to build.

---

* For these experiments, rats are better than mice. We know more about how rats think and learn.

† OK, it wasn't really a race, but I think of it that way in my mind.

What's the scale of the need in neurobiology?
Today, 50 million people worldwide suffer from epilepsy and 80 million undergo the scourge of Alzheimer's. For the year 2005, the market for treating Alzheimer's Disease alone is pegged at $4 billion.

The neurobiology data on humans is scarce indeed. So our ventures are exploratory. The market experience is that these compounds are licensed to pharmaceutical companies in very early stages of development. For all of these complex diseases, there is no single magic pill, and we certainly don't pretend to have it. What will overcome devastating disease is the collective force of a million small insights and breakthroughs.

Not only have we become one small, interconnected world, we have also become one carefully interconnected global intelligence. That's what the science networks of the future will be all about.

Who are the brains behind ABS?
The Pharmacology Professor Dr Gustav Born at the William Harvey Research Institute in London (son of Nobel Laureate Max Born) was probably the first Global Scientific Network member of truly world stature. He and I first met at a conference at Harvard, and I could see instantly that ABS would benefit from Gus's vast wisdom and considerable analytical skills. Both he and his father before him were dedicated networkers on an international dimension. I asked Gus to join our Board, and I was honoured when he said yes. He taught me the value of simplicity when he rejected my first offer to him and sent

back the 25-page consulting agreement my lawyer had mailed him, and we exchanged one-page letters instead.

The Born family has taught all of us plenty about courage — the way his father rallied world scientists at the Pugwash Conferences and elsewhere to oppose German rearmament; and the way his niece, Olivia Newton-John, has battled back against cancer.

Our Network includes so many distinguished scientists, I'm especially proud of the way in which they have learned to work together — alternately challenging and supporting each other as the situation requires. That's often not the case in the sciences. Recently, I heard about two supposed collaborators who, I am glad to say, are not part of our team. The pharmacologist called the chemist an idiot. The pharmacologist's gripe: the chemist was too lazy to design a compound without a nitrogen atom in it!

That's like an art critic blasting a painter for leaning on his blues too much, or a food connoisseur lambasting a chef who can cook only sauces with beef stock in them. Fortunately, we have very agile chemists like Professor Jacob Szmuszkovicz, the Retired Distinguished Scientist from Upjohn, and Professor Heinz Nau, Chairman of the Department of Food Toxicology in the School of Veterinary Medicine in Hanover.

Dr Ciaran Regan is Professor in the Department of Pharmacology at University College Dublin. Both he and Heinz Nau are dear friends and brilliant scientists, but they are also a partnership that has been fostered within the Network. In this duo, Heinz is the chemist and Ciaran the biologist. They have extensive interaction with each other, and their names stand side-by-side on one patent. They — and their universities — will share in the royalties of what they create. Most importantly, they get along well with each other, and enjoy tackling a challenge.

Signing Up a Scientist

Usually, the scientist is both the least expensive *and* the most important part of a high-technology project. The same challenge faces me as faced the dukes and archbishops who bankrolled scientists and scholars during the Renaissance. You really have to understand *how* a scientist's mind works, even though you may not understand *what* that mind is working on in a profound way.

- *Track down the needs for self-esteem and approval.* Scientists must have the drive to prove something, accomplish something, be involved in something.

- *Pay attention to the tone of voice and the body language.* Is it urgent and pressing forward? Does the person have an insatiable need to achieve?

- *Spotlight the work.* Generally, the last thing scientists ask is, 'What's the pay?' The usual priority is: 'What's the work and who are my collaborators?' Often, they hold out until they read and study the published papers by their potential colleagues. According to Professor Ciaran Regan, 'Scientists live off buzz.' They are motivated by high-energy involvement with exciting work in progress.

- *Find the collaborative instinct.* Can this person work with others? Are they enthusiastic about sharing ideas? Can they partner-up to a common goal?

- *Don't be a business know-it-all:* Highly educated scientists often feel intimidated that they don't have a command of business. Use the soft-touch to let them know competent people are handling the pounds and dollars, while the scientists do the job they're best at.

A biologist like Ciaran will always feel that he is not getting the compounds he likes or not in enough quantity. A chemist like Heinz will be frustrated that the biologist is not evaluating compounds quickly enough. Heinz is interested in modelling the compounds, not in synthesising them by the truckload. The chemist has to figure out how to build the molecule and which glues will be used to hold it together. The chemist produces and the biologist evaluates. And then they turn the tables on each other. But between Ciaran and Heinz it's all done with such grace, camaraderie and, above all, *respect*. That's what makes it special and what makes it work.

If one message about managing the sciences of the future deserves top billing and if there is one lesson I have learned through ABS, it is that women will be every bit the equal of men in the sciences and the science businesses of the future. Throughout history, women have been trained to be better thinkers, more patient, shrewder, and better able to spot the meaning behind the meaning. They're more tenacious, more persistent, and more detail-oriented. Women will be best qualified to run the companies and countries of the future because they run the basic unit — the family. They know every problem any organisation will ever have. In my view, it's time to go beyond giving women equality and to start encouraging men to emulate the brainpower traits of women.

What is the prototype of the woman manager in the coming century? To answer that, I need only describe the characteristics of one woman — Ellena Byrne in Dublin, who is Executive Vice-President of ABS and who charts the direction of the ABS Global Network, a network she more than anyone has been responsible for building. So often she has said to me when I was about to throw in the towel on a project, 'Mr Roach, they're getting so close.' She has really helped me anchor my commitment to this business. Ellena is perseverance personified.

The Ellena Prototype

- *Able to inter-relate and communicate at all levels.* Not a scientist (although more able than many in the broader conceptual realm), and a master of converting scientific communication to clear, intelligent, layman's language.

- *An anticipatory planner:* Mothers are the greatest anticipators in the world.

- *Willing to share the spotlight.* She works with leading scientists (who can be very headstrong at times), and is always the first to credit that achievements belong to others. She is modest and also smart enough to know how to keep the ball rolling.

- *Information literate.* Ellena exerts influence through telecommunications and the computer. She also works from home. The personal computer has become the work bench of the future. No more will hammers and swords dominate work or government. This changing balance of power will permit the brainpower of women to dominate.

- *An agile negotiator:* Able to deal fairly with people of all cultures in a way that makes them anxious to act positively in the common interest.

- *Compassionate.* A home to stray cats — some beautiful ones. But she also has an enlightened compassion for human beings. She understands how to match people-with-needs with problems that need solution. This is a much richer sense of opportunity than found in most clumsy male-oriented solutions.

An outstanding example of professional leadership at ABS, Ellena is not alone. We are blessed with several women of a similar calibre, and I admire all of them. And, they all seem to live by the same truth:

> Brainpower rules; muscle power, fire power, and flower power can't match it.

10

What Will the Children Ask?

Beginning with a visit to China in 1979, Al was immediately comfortable in the role of being a business ambassador and informal statesman in a world with an increasingly global character. Colleagues have emphasised his skill in getting along with people at all social and economic levels and of every cultural and national background.

Al's knack for achieving understanding and consensus in complex situations was dramatised in 1990 at a senior policy conference in Russia, where, in a spontaneous speech, he asserted that Russia and its people — a nation and a culture that had contributed so much to the advance of human history — deserved support and respect in making the transition to becoming a democracy and market economy.

Al's practice of personally paying for full-page editorial open letters has continued through the 1990s with an increasing emphasis on the risks posed by nuclear weapons, especially after the Cold War ended and nuclear arsenals in the one-time Eastern Bloc fell into disrepair and became the targeted booty of terrorists and criminals. He first urged the creation of a Marshall-like Plan to help stabilise the Russian economic situation in 1993, astutely wary of charity versus direct human help.

In the five years since, he has reinforced his message on the need for nuclear responsibility by emphasising that the children of the future will hold our generations accountable for poor policies or negligence or for any tragedy that maims humanity for centuries. It is we who will be responsible if such policies or negligence lead to the utter annihilation of our planet.

'Is that you, Nellie?'

I'm lying in my bed, and it's four o'clock in the morning. Tigger — a mouser with seven formidable claws on each mighty paw — has just brushed my face. He must have. Who else? 'Cat, give me a break,' I moan.

Then I look over at the window-sill far across the room, and there's Tigger curled up, fast asleep, and certainly not dumb enough to get up at four o'clock in the morning so he could stick his paw in my face. 'Nellie, is that you?'

In minutes I'm on the phone to Moscow, where it's twelve noon. Professor Peter Morozov answers. Peter, an eminent psychiatrist (a second generation psychiatrist in a family of three generations of psychiatrists and four generations of doctors),* is the editor of Russia's leading medical journal, a ten-year veteran of the World Health Organisation, and a member of our ABS staff in Russia. The discussion is animated; and, in it, I dissect how we intend to market one of our cardiovascular products in Russia. For days I have struggled with the problem, and suddenly the answer hit me in my sleep. Or maybe it brushed me in my sleep.

It's not until ten minutes after the call, as I stand in my kitchen overlooking the reedy shoreline in the yard of my Long Island home, that I think again about the brush I felt with my head on the pillow. Hurling fruits and vitamin supplements into a food processor, concocting what friends have dubbed *Roach's rocket fuel*, I am then certain that it *was* Nellie. My mother Nellie.

Often, when a business problem has contorted every

---

* In 1989, Dr Peter Morozov was a leader in his profession in taking a stand that the Soviet government had used psychiatry as a tool of political intimidation. His family has a knack for innovation. His grandfather was a virologist who in 1953 received a state prize for the creation of a dry vaccine against small pox.

nerve in my body and nearly extinguished the fire in my gut, I'll sleep on it, and Nellie will stream through my subconscious like a rush of smart energy. Everything will suddenly be clear. I swear I can feel the *whoooosh*. There is a presence: Hi, Mom.

How do flashes of brilliance and moments of great insight happen? Are individuals always responsible for their own genius or do we intersect with forces beyond our control? Neurobiologists tell us our understanding of how the mind works is tiny. How do we know that when the mind works it works alone?

When life humbles me, I recall standing on the Great Wall of China. When the astronauts landed on the moon, the only two man-made landmarks they could identify were the Sphinx in Egypt and the Great Wall. When I walked the Wall, I asked our tour guide if the wall achieved what it was built to do. Nope. 'When the Manchu invaders penetrated China and conquered the Ming Dynasty, they just bribed a traitor to open the gate,' he explained.

That knowledge makes you put even the grandest of human achievements and the most methodical plans into perspective. Not only may the finest ideas come from incomprehensible sources, but our grandest designs are usually flawed.

I first visited China in 1979. My hope was to bring fresh-water shrimp farming there. China has had a well-developed fish-farming culture for centuries. Government aeroplanes took me all around China to lecture top intellectuals on aquaculture, water purification and disinfection.

When I was asked questions, they would begin translating my answers into Chinese. Inevitably, someone would stand up and say: 'That translation isn't right.'

Then, they paid me a great compliment. The senior official in the room stood up and said, 'Mr Roach, you just speak English. There will be no translation.'

Most of them understood English, and I think probably understood me better without a professional translator tampering in the middle. They needed no interpreter for me or for Nixon, who had indeed made my trip possible.

Richard Nixon's historic trip to China in February 1972 opened a 'forbidden gate' for American businesses. Nixon may have been vilified at home in the States in those years right after Watergate, but in China he was regarded nearly as a god. During my 1979 trip, *Investment Dealers' Digest* invited me to contribute a by-lined report of my findings. 'A very high regard is placed upon learning in both the technical and classical fields,' I wrote, and I described the cities as 'scrupulously clean', the population as 'well fed' and 'imbued with a sense of purpose'. I also observed that there were a mere '3,000,000 telephones throughout the nation or about one telephone per every 333 people'. Some folks look at the number of cars in the driveway or the size of the house as signs of prosperity and opportunity. Me? I count telephones.*

When I recently read Paul Sweeney's *The Celtic Tiger*, I was intrigued to read that Ireland has risen to be among the top twenty nations in the world as regards mobile phone saturation.† What a commercial opportunity for

---

* Roach, Alfred J., 'A Businessman's Impressions of China as it is Today', *Investment Dealers' Digest*, 1 May 1979.

† Sweeney, Paul, *The Celtic Tiger: Ireland's Economic Miracle Explained*, Dublin: Oak Tree Press, 1998, p. 52.

telecommunications China remains. As of 1998, it plans to invest $100 billion in telecommunications in the coming years. TII is proud of its evolving partnership with Shanghai Tel and with Shanghai University — the most renowned technical university in China. Obviously, this will become the largest new market for surge-protection equipment in the world.

My admiration for Chinese culture is great, especially the respect shown to the old and the young. In China, the respect is really directed at the living family, more than at departed ancestors, as is widely believed. I remember once seeing a family surround an older lady at a restaurant and serve her as she silently pointed to *shumais* or prawns or rice balls in the centre of the table. None of them would have thought of eating until her whole plate was composed. At the end of the meal, everyone rose and she led the march out. People talk up a storm about human rights. But how about human respect? How can you beat such a show of respect? The respect in China works in both directions: to small children as much as elders. In my opinion, the robust family tradition in China helped them weather Communism.

Chinese law has been an enigma for us Westerners, especially on two scores. The first is punishment dished out for crimes. China is a disciplined society. Capital punishment is applied more often than in any other country in the world.* The bullet in the back of the head, often in a stadium in front of massive crowds, is swift and brutal. I have witnessed the violent precursor to this practice in the streets of Shanghai as early as 1936. Yet the remarkable safety I feel on the streets of the teeming cities,

---

* Amnesty International recorded 4,300 executions in China in 1996 — more than in any country in the world (Russia has put a hold on executions for some time now). Even in China, the number is on the decline, per a television report in February 1998.

makes me wonder about the Western indictment of this practice. Perhaps capital punishment is so staunchly imbedded because the legal profession was nearly wiped out. When China followed the advice in Shakespeare's *Henry VI*, and killed all the lawyers — in its case as a by-product of Communism and 'cultural' reform — Chinese contracts were paralysed for decades. Without contracts, how could they export?

Token Taken

In 1994, we signed a contract with a prestigious Chinese scientific organisation. At the ceremony, I reached inside my suit for a pen only to discover there was none in my pocket.

'Ciaran, lend me your pen,' I whispered to my ABS colleague Professor Ciaran Regan, from University College Dublin. I had just given him an expensive Mont Blanc pen shortly before the visit.

My counterpart signed first and handed me his pen as a gesture of friendship. What was I to do, except hand the co-signator my pen? I thought Ciaran was going to have a heart attack! Later he told me his thoughts at that moment: 'My God, he's taking my little treasure!'

It was a pleasure to give the pen. The replacement pen I gave to Ciaran was even better than the one he had before, but I later learned that the pen I had given him was itself a memento of an historic signing — a cornerstone agreement between University College Dublin and ABS. The whole experience taught me a deep truth: never go into an international signing ceremony with an empty holster.

What has happened to Russia is as astonishing as the re-make of China but different in very important ways. In 1990, I was in Leningrad for a meeting of a distinguished council of leading American business people, which sometimes functioned as a kitchen cabinet to US presidents. It was just at the time of the Great Change, when they were re-christening the town St Petersburg. President Gorbachev was in power, but the winds were clearly shifting towards democracy.

During one of my visits to Russia with the International Policy Forum, a remarkable Russian scholar from St Petersburg addressed us. Very heroic and equally clear-thinking is how I remember her. She was a PhD in international political science, and spoke several languages as well as an impressive array of Russian dialects. Her remarks that afternoon were in perfect English. Her short talk was a bull's-eye and brought the session to an emotional peak. Here's how I remember her message:

> We didn't want to be, but all of us in the Soviet Union were scared. One can never understand what fear is until you are involved in it. As an intellectual, who had the chance to go to university and see the outside world, I had a taste of freedom. But, the fear still seized us.
>
> Until very recent months, I and my family ... and many of us in Russia ... have known nothing else but fear. I remember sitting in the evening with my family or friends — making small talk or watching TV, and then... [*Wham — wham, she banged on the podium with her fist. Everyone in the audience bolted upright. Our speaker's voice tightened up into an ominous whisper*] ... just like you did, that's how we all would react when we heard that knock. A knock on the door. It is the most terrible occurrence one could imagine. You will never know how quickly the natural warmth of a family circle can dissolve into sheer terror. We would all turn to each other as we tried to figure out what that knock might portend. Instantly the cold

fear would overtake you, and your hair would stand on end. Which one of us may disappear? For how long?

Fortunately, for me, the knock at the door never meant anything more than a stray visitor or a neighbour looking for a cup of flour.

Perhaps you'll understand why we ask that you be patient with us ... because we're coming out of the dark. That abject fear has thrust us into darkness. And, we have been in the dark for seventy years. When you have been in the dark for that long, the light is bound to make you blink and to cause you to make mistakes. What we are looking for, quite simply, is your guidance — your advice and counsel on how we handle freedom. We don't know how a free market works. You must understand we need teachers and patient guides, not handouts. Thank you.

When she finished, there was a deep silence in the room.

Then the nay-sayers started in and all but ignored her appeal. First a vice-president from an international bank delivered an arrogant tirade about how the Russians couldn't be trusted and that money sent to Russia would be poured into a black hole. Then a televangelist got up and suggested that the Russians were Antichrists and not to be trusted. Next, a lawyer counted off all the legal and administrative risks that would doubtless result from reaching out to the Russians. All three made the Russians look like hapless beggars at the door of Western civilisation, who hadn't made a single contribution to humanity.

Rage boiled inside me. I looked at the Russian woman and could see her sinking down in her chair, and the old bully-fighting instincts surfaced in a flash. The rest of the Russians were staring woodenly down at the conference table. I couldn't restrain myself, and I asked for the floor — in fact, I demanded it. The panel chairman apologised and said that the agenda had only forty seconds left. Then I spun around and shot a steely glance at the president of the organisation. He said resolutely, 'Give him the time.'

When I reached the podium, my heart wrested control from my mind. Turning to the Russian woman, I said:

Madam, you have just witnessed an expression of freedom as *we* know it in the United States.

Since you asked for help on handling freedom, let me offer some ... and an assurance besides. While the people you have just heard may use impressive terms and draw their conclusions with absolute certainty, they do not speak for the United States. They speak only for themselves. Speaking for *myself*, I wish to disassociate myself from their remarks and I want to further assure you that *their* attitudes are not those of the political, social, religious, and business leaders in America — not those whom I know, and I know many distinguished ones.

The American opinion leaders I am fortunate enough to know are committed to giving the Russian people advice as well as economic support, even though you personally did not ask for financial aid in your comments.

What our own people sometimes forget is that freedom is neither a gift nor an entitlement. It is a trust. And, it is a trust which must be wisely exercised. One must not only speak freely, but speak responsibly as well.

These last speakers are addressing you as though Russia were a basket case. Neither Russia, nor its people — believe me — are a basket case.

The suggestion that Russia has not contributed to world civilisation is preposterous. You have given the world some of the greatest scientists the world has ever seen. Writers like Tolstoy and Dostoevsky stand among the very giants of world literature. Such composers as Tchaikovsky and Rachmaninoff have penned some of the most beautiful music ever known.

You have built one of the greatest scientific and military powerhouses in human history. You were in space before we were. First through Sputnik, and then with Cosmonaut Yuri Gagarin, you set the pace for space exploration and made us your grudging admirers for years. Thank God you woke us up and gave us a goal.

In medicine, you achieved the first blood transfusion and pioneered the microsurgery needed to reconnect severed limbs.* You were the first in countless other medical breakthroughs. Russia need never apologise for its contribution to the world community.

Russia and the United States must put pettiness to bed. Setting the Bible's guidance in modern terms, it is now time to pound those nuclear swords into ploughshares and to make that the foundation of a market economy. It can and will be done. Let's work together to build a better world for our grandchildren. Thank you for your speech and your appeal, and I hope that my colleagues here will have the good grace and good sense to take what you said here deep to heart.

The room was absolutely silent. I wasn't sure if I had just scored a triumph or triggered a catastrophe. Then, there was thunderous applause, and the Russian scholar bounded over to me and gave me a terrific hug. The televangelist's reaction was a classic. He ambled over and slapped my back, saying, 'If you could only speak for *God* like you just spoke for the people of Russia, I'd like to have you on my TV show.'

The Russians have endured so much. They are a people who have freed themselves without great violence, but they have done so with huge economic sacrifices. It has caused some to ravage their dignity and others to preserve it with great style.

---

* The first blood transfusion was achieved by Dr Andrei Martinovich Wolff in the city of St Petersburg in 1832. Many will remember the pioneering microsurgery work done by Professor Demikhov who stunned the world with the successful transplantation of a dog head onto the body of another living dog, which was such a breakthrough that it later enabled transplantation of human organs, such as hearts.

Not far from the Bolshoi Theatre one evening, I met an officer on the streets in Russia who wanted to sell me his boots. 'Mister, give me couple a dollars,' he pleaded in tortured English. 'I got couple kids. Family wants eat.'

I gave him twenty dollars and told him to keep his boots. He insisted I take them, and I told him to keep his goddamn boots, and I stomped away with tears streaming down my face. The boot encounter was bad enough, but I have witnessed far worse.

A little guy — blond and about seven years old — came up to me on Red Square, 'For one Yankee dollar, I will ...' When you have grandchildren of the same age, your gut turns quickly. There is no fire at such a moment — just a deep and empty feeling of sorrow. Yet again I was seeing the hopeless poverty I saw and heard hopping trains in the US during the Great Depression, and later at the harbour of Dakar — same degradation, different accent.

I also saw scarcity handled with remarkable dignity and ingenuity. In St Petersburg, we hosted a dinner for a group of medical and technical people in the dining room of the Grand Hotel Europe — one of the most luxurious hotels in the city.

A stained-glass window dominates one entire wall of the huge, high-ceilinged dining room, which resembles a cathedral more than a restaurant. On the side were handsomely draped alcoves where you could pull a rich brocade curtain and create a private dining room. A string quartet seated on the gallery above played the *Andante Cantabile* from Tchaikovsky's first string quartet — at least that's what our waiter told me it was when I asked him.

Perhaps a few Russian entrepreneurs who had struck it rich, or a sprinkling of gangster bosses, could afford dinner at a restaurant like this, but it was well beyond the reach of even the medical profession. Two nights later, one of the Russians reciprocated with a buffet in his apartment, but not on his own. One of the guests brought a ham. Another brought *piroshkis*, and a third came with a steaming pot of borscht. And there was glass after frosty glass of vodka. It was a banquet second to none, which no one of them could have afforded to present *alone*. Our feast reminded me of sharing in our Harlem apartment house. Even in a free-enterprise economy, certain collective approaches make sense.

I find the Russians and the Irish alike in many ways. They laugh the same way. They enjoy a good scrap. They're quick to anger and quick to make up. Both peoples become sentimental easily. When I'm at a banquet or a concert and I look at their features, after a while I see my Uncle Luke and my Aunt Bridget. And, then there are the hordes of people with red hair in both countries.

Still, there is a problem with Russia and the regions once tyrannised by the Soviet Union. And, it's a big one: over 21,000 absurdly useless nuclear weapons — enough fire power to incinerate every living creature on the face of the earth — lie in silos spread over Russia and its adjacent republics. Without a doubt, this is the most dangerous case of human-inflicted garbage in history.

This call to control the risk of the discarded weaponry of the Cold War was triggered personally when my granddaughter Stacey came into my study with eight-month-old Robbie poised on her arm. He was napping peacefully, but Stacey looked pensive. She asked me, 'What kind of world, Grandfather, can my child expect to grow up in?'

In May 1997, I wrote another open editorial piece which appeared in the *International Herald Tribune*, entitled 'What Will the Children Ask? Reflections on the Marshall Plan and our Future'* In it, I anticipated what

---

* The Marshall Plan, named after former US Secretary of State George C. Marshall, provided important funding to help the reconstruction of ravaged Western Europe after the Second World War.

children like my great-grandson Robbie might ask in twenty years, if the advanced economies of the world did not collaborate in financing a Marshall-like Plan for the stabilisation of Russia.

> 'You mean world leaders couldn't see that the intelligentsia of Russia's enormous military and scientific establishment were cut loose from jobs and opportunities and that a critical few would sell skills and materials to the highest bidder?'

> 'You're telling us that no one foresaw that the East Bloc nuclear arsenal offered exactly the weapons that terrorist groups and rogue nations wanted desperately to command?'

> 'You're asking us to believe that a large piece of the world became a contaminated, radioactive cinder because we weren't smart enough to fund a transition to post-Cold War peace?'

Oh boy. Why did this episode with Stacey trouble me so? Because it had happened before. My daughter Dorothy is a gifted mathematician and physicist who worked at one of the arsenals and probably worked on atomic weapons. After she was married for several years, I asked her why there were no grandchildren. She said, 'Dad, I don't want to bring children into a world where they will probably be incinerated.'

From that day forward, I became a campaigner against the madness that nuclear weapons could unleash, especially now that those weapons serve no strategic purpose whatever. I am not the first to write cautioning letters to the world. In 1955, Albert Einstein, Max Born, and Bertrand Russell, with six other Nobel Laureate scientists issued a manifesto warning that an 'H-Bomb war might put an end to the human race'. Even as I write, a nuclear arms race between India and Pakistan imperils the Indian subcontinent. The world, it seems, needs constant reminders.

To the readers, I explained that the cost of a new Marshall-like plan for Russia would be minimal. And I emphasised that if we do not act now, our neglect could catapult us into parallel disasters. A nation with demanding internal priorities may be hard-pressed to safeguard super-weapons from the ravages of decay. Such a country could equally become easy prey to global nuclear pirates. George Marshall may have been a distinguished humanitarian. But, in my opinion, he made a greater contribution to humanity because he was something more: a dedicated pragmatist.

I made sure my message didn't evaporate. So many vital messages do. In another open letter in January 1998, entitled 'What Fate Awaits Our World's Children?' I called upon world leaders to:

- Stimulate our best organisational and diplomatic thinkers to find ways to ensure that strategic nuclear substances are always in the hands of reliable authorities, totally committed to world peace;

- Devise new and more reliable methods to monitor and detect existing nuclear weapons everywhere;

- Challenge scientists globally to devise more cost-effective ways to convert today's nuclear stockpile into harmless substances or beneficial resources.

And I invited the scientists of the world to develop alternative technologies to prevent the production of weapons-grade materials in existing power plants. Perhaps the most exciting development in modern science is the evolution of replacement reactor technologies that may prevent the production of weapons-grade fissionable material. One of the finest minds in physics is at work on the challenge, and I am in regular contact with him.

The nuclear trauma always makes me think of my grandchildren. I have nine at the moment, along with three great-grandchildren and they are treasures to my heart. We are up against a whole new world of grandparenting. The game is not what it used to be — not some brief interlude between retirement and burial. With such dramatic changes in life expectancy, do we know what to do with ourselves and how we intervene in other people's lives? We don't know a damn thing about doing it right.

Grandparenting. I asked Stacey, a budget analyst by profession, 'How should a grandparent, or great-grandparent give guidance to their offspring?' Her suggestions are in 'The Gramps Guide' opposite.

What is the real future we all face? That's no easy matter. God has to be one hell of a physics professor. Bacteria may live for seconds and mayflies for a day. But, humans? I must be the product of some sort of evolution. I think back to my earliest days in Harlem. With short legs, I couldn't run that fast. And fighting hurt like hell. So I learned to talk. Most of all I learned to think. You start that way and after a while one idea possesses you: enjoy every day because there may not be another.

A neuro-scientist in Tel Aviv told me a tale, and it's proof positive that God is one heck of an investment banker: In the Sinai, three young entrepreneurs on pilgrimage are visited by an apparition. It's the Master himself.

'Lord, what's a million light years to you?' the first asks.

'Just a minute,' He answers.

'What's a million dollars to you?' asks the second.

'Hardly a penny.'

The third and boldest tries to close the deal, 'Lord, can we borrow a million dollars?'

The desert rumbles with the Master's huge sigh, 'Sure ... in just a minute.'

The Gramps Guide

- *Don't fret about today's fix — teach kids how to solve problems in general.* How dumb are we grandparents? Very. What happened yesterday is doubtless going to happen again next year or the year after. You name the issue. You teach little when you find the fast answer to get out of today's fix and don't have the guidelines for making decisions long term.

- *Be there for your grandchildren, when nobody else is, even when they don't deserve to have someone there.* Tell them to call you when they feel they can call no one. *No matter what!* You're tough enough to take a hard call. I've told them, 'Got trouble? Call me. I've heard everything.' Hell, if you haven't, you're reading the wrong book.

- *Save your 'Don't you wish you dids...' for later.* They won't learn in the heat of battle. Who does? Did you? Wait for the right moment. Not the instant that gives you the greatest satisfaction ('Ah-hah, you little fool, I told you so'), but the one that imprints the right message long term.

- *Be a friend, more than an adult.* Don't try to solve problems as the *resident adult*. Help as a human being. Caught in a similar jam, what would you do — *really* do?

What will my legacy be? I never thought I'd make more than thirty thousand dollars. I've made millions. But in the end it doesn't matter. There are two great legacies people can leave behind. The first is to help bring humanity to

its senses when it has lost its way. I hope I've done my
share on the rebuilding of Eastern Europe and on the
hazards of the rotting nuclear arsenal. The second legacy
is doing something you really don't have to do. Great
artists and athletes do that. Scholars and spiritual leaders do it, too. Doing something for the pure pleasure of it
— wow, that's something!

So much of my life has been spent doing things I didn't
really have to do. What fun! Experimenting or achieving
or doing my best to inspire others — that gives me a kick.
Professor Gus Born once told a friend of mine: 'Al Roach
has added an enormous amount of fun to my life.' Who
couldn't live (or die) with an epitaph like that?

In 1997, Malcolm W. Browne wrote in *The New York
Times*:

> ... a team of Dutch and American astronomers ... had de-
> tected and analyzed light from a galaxy lying some 13 billion
> light years away — light that began its voyage when the
> universe was only about 7 percent of its present age.*

In 1998, astronomers witnessed the biggest explosion
ever with the exception of the Big Bang. When did it
happen? Twelve billion light years ago ... and we humans
just got the news a month ago. These reports reminded
me of a passage from a poem by my friend Stephen Doak:

> The stars twinkle their white light,
> ever so old but then so new;
> their light comes from history
> all so innocent to us.

When life exits, the soul takes off. Don't confine what's
left to some mouldy tomb. Flesh won't endure eternity,
and I don't like the leather look of Egyptian mummies. I

---

* Browne, Malcolm W., 'A Sight of the Infant Universe', *New York
Times*, 3 August 1997.

want to be cremated, taken up into the air, and launched over the Irish Sea or maybe over Dorado Bay in Puerto Rico, where I can visualise some young lovelies in their bikinis scratching away that puff of air-borne Roach dust. My mother once said: 'Alfred, you won't be in heaven and you won't be in hell.'

She may be right. Perhaps I'll be doing the limbo for eternity. I'll just be a ball of energy whistling around. Lord, let me frolic with those spirits who have stoked the love in my heart and the fire in my belly.

Appendices

1

Volcanoes

The following is my own personal health programme. I designed it myself, after doing a lot of research, consulting a lot of experts, and taking into account my own physical condition. You should not follow it or any part of it without consulting your own doctor(s).

'Dancing on a Volcano' — That's how the Comte de Salvandy put it in 1830. He was talking about European politics, but for me it's a way of summing up the drama and energy of life. On the bad side, dancing on the volcano is flagrantly toying with the nightmare of thermonuclear disaster. On the good side, it's the unleashed energy we have within us.

Any book about bellies should have an appendix, and here's mine. How did an old cuss like me get to live so long and still have so much spunk in me? I attribute much of it to my philosophy of wellness, and I summarise the key ingredients of that philosophy in one word: *volcanoes*.

Why volcanoes? Because volcanoes are the greatest natural fire bellies in all the world. Volcanoes are not to be toyed with. In 1902, when the volcano on the island of Martinique exploded, 26,000 people were killed. Fire in the belly? Make way for Mother Nature. When Mount Kilauea erupts in Hawaii, the lava reaches a temperature of 1,200 degrees Celsius. When Mount St Helen's exploded in May 1980, it released the energy of a 400 megaton atomic bomb, eight times the power of any atomic bomb ever exploded (and I dearly hope ever will be exploded).

Here's my version of volcanoes and what they mean to me.

V-itamins: The older you get, the harder it is to produce and absorb the vitamins and minerals you need daily. Everyone's nutrition-supplement requirements differ. With meals each day, I consume a power dose of vitamins that ranges from milk thistle to ginkgo biloba to beta-carotene.

O-xygen: Deep breathing is how I welcome each day. Head out the window. Oxygen in, carbon dioxide out. Aware and expansive breathing makes anyone more alert and releases tension. You inhale 11 to 12 thousand times a day. Might as well learn how to do it right.

L-aughter: As Max Beerbohm told us, no 'one is known in history or legend as having died of laughter' and many — I believe — have lived the longer for it. Laughter is not the sacred province of the great joke or the master comic. It is the willingness to see the positive and amusing opportunities in the world around you.

C-ayenne: When I say fire in my belly, I truly mean it. I take six pepper capsules a day. They generate a quarter of a million heat units! Man, I sprinkle the stuff in my bath, and, if I scrape my elbow, I turn cayenne into a salve. From ulcers to the common cold, cayenne can heal more ills than penicillin, I firmly believe, and wise ancient cultures from China to Senegal have harnessed its power properties.

A-nimation: Say it with feeling. Do it with feeling. Life is challenging. Many nights, I go to bed just before midnight, saying, 'That's it! I'm retiring.' But I usually fall asleep with the conviction: 'If I'm alive in the morning, I'll be in at eight.'

N-utrition: I don't eat right always, but I eat right often. The healthiest part of what I've learned about nutrition and wellness is something I must credit the Pritikin Longevity Center with. Lots of vegetables and fruits. Plenty of fibre. And, even when I stray, I have a recipe for Irish-Mist-spiked avocado dip that Paul Newman would die for.

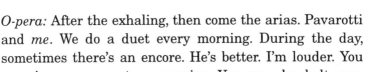

O-pera: After the exhaling, then come the arias. Pavarotti and *me.* We do a duet every morning. During the day, sometimes there's an encore. He's better. I'm louder. You can sing your way to expression. You can also belt your way to superior stress control.

E-limination: One day each week, I detoxify myself using the same psyllium seed and ground flax seed that thoroughbred breeders give to $25 million race horses. A stud is a stud, the way I figure it.

S-tretching: When I climb out of a car, I say to myself 'Come on old buddy, you can make it.' and I do. Intelligent stretching will be the athletic art form of the coming century, as more and more people have post-80 demographics as I do.

Were I to elaborate, it might require another book and perhaps another book it will be. I don't want to explore all my wellness philosophies, but I would like to talk about just three: cayenne, opera, and stretching.

Cayenne: Roach's Rocket Fuel

My infatuation with cayenne pepper began in Senegal in the 1970s, where they have very spicy foods. Gambia, right next to it, was colonised by the English, who don't like spicy food. Researchers found that there was a high incidence of colon and oesophageal cancer in Gambia, but not in Senegal. People in both nations eat a lot of fish, rice, and couscous, but the cayenne pepper was the critical void in the Gambian diet.

We in the industrialised West are members of what I call the CDN — the Cayenne Deprived Nations. I take six pepper capsules a day. That generates a quarter of a million heat units. A cold? Not for me. No germ can live with me. Cayenne can also make you very romantic, or at least that's my opinion. Sometimes I put cayenne pepper right in my bath. In Tiajuana, I busted open a cayenne capsule and sprinkled it on my tamales and rice. The owner of the café rushed over, waving his arms like a matador. He thought I was spiking the food with LSD or *peyote*. Only when I put a dab on his forefinger and made him taste it, did he say '*La pimienta está bien condimentada*. Si, si, señor and enjoy your dinner.'

Several experts say that some people swallow capsules to shrink haemorrhoids. The therapy is not exactly pleasant because the cayenne can burn powerfully when it departs you, but some say it works. Anyone with high blood pressure should not take cayenne without consulting a doctor.

We now know that ulcers are caused by bacteria. I'm convinced that cayenne could have saved me from having a large portion of my stomach removed in 1954. I have used cayenne as a salve on tissue recovering from a bad abrasion or the removal of a malignant skin mole, but don't treat any aspect of a malignancy without involving a doctor first.

Cayenne is effective because it is powerful and so it deserves respect. I would suggest that anyone consult their doctor before taking it on a regular basis. For those who wish to read more about the benefits, I recommend Sam Biser's book, *Curing with Cayenne*, which features Dr Richard Schulze.

Opera: Singing Along with Signor Pavarotti

In 1998, I made my début on Russian television on a programme with a regular viewership of about 80 million. It was a programme on aging, and I was one of the guests. Another was the similarly aged retiring director of the opera company at the Bolshoi Theatre. The show pieced together our interview segments. He declined to sing, but not me. No sir. I belted out my window-pane rattling imitation of Pavarotti.

Why do I sing? Because it *makes* me feel good. Not because I already feel good. After my deep-breathing exercises, and before I jump in the pool, I sing loudly and emotionally. I consume oxygen by the tank-car load. My worries, frustrations and anger evaporate. My concentration is dedicated. But every day, it's a war of nerves and stamina. Will I be able to hold that high note as long as that Italian guy can? Usually it's a draw. My housekeeper Barbara now knows not to interrupt me during those high-pressure moments.

Stretching: Tigger, Tigger, Stretching Teacher

In every section of this book where I offer advice outside my direct expertise, I have consulted the best experts in the discipline, such as Irene O'Mahoney, a first-rate physical therapist. So it is with stretching, and my stretching ace is a twelve-year-old mouser by the name of Tigger. This tiger-striped tabby turned up one day, and he has permitted me to live with him ever since. If seven cat years are equivalent to a single human one, then Tigger is two years older than I am — roughly 84 in human terms.

Watch Tigger in the Kitchen

Cat movements have intrigued me since I was in the Fire Department and saw cats crawl out of blazes that humans didn't survive because the cats had the sense to crouch close to the ground. Watch a cat stretching after it has been asleep. It flexes every muscle in its body, down to the tail and the ears as well. Does it work? I don't know if Tigger can leap tall buildings in a single bound, but he can jump five times his height to reach the kitchen sink, and he does it often. Unbeatable advice, and all it cost me was a tummy massage and a tin of salmon!

Watch Al Roach on an Aeroplane
'My, you do stretch a lot,' has been said to me often by fellow passengers on long flights. It's second nature to me. 'Remarkable. You stretched only five times on that walk to the nose of the plane as opposed to the usual eight,' an insomniac Englishman once said on a flight to Cairo. I'll do it anywhere — in the middle of meetings, during interviews, on the Great Wall, or in the narrow aisle of a 747. Hey, flight attendant, where's my salmon? After all, if I asked for the tummy tickle, she might get the wrong idea.

Appendix 2

Open Letter as it appeared in
The New York Times
Sunday, 24 January 1982

An urgent message to
the President and the Congress
of the United States of America

Dear Mr. President:

Fear!

Not since Franklin D. Roosevelt told our nation, 'The only thing we have to fear is fear itself', has fear gripped so many of our people. We Americans responded to President Roosevelt's remarks with deep faith and great determination. We built the mightiest industrial and military complex known to man. And we went on to victory.

War With Japan — Then and Now

Four decades ago we went to war with Japan, following 'the day of infamy' at Pearl Harbor. Today we are again at war with Japan — this time an undeclared economic war — and the outlook is grim. I am not against Japan's prosperity. But I am outraged that it is *they* who are prospering at *our* expense; especially when we consider Japan's broad economic programs; organizing government, industry, labor, education and banking with the objective of full employment for the Japanese people. At the same time, our Government appears bent on destroying our economy. We have nine million, four hundred thousand unemployed people. Japan has virtually none.

Japan's Strategy

Japan does not hide its strategy for winning the economic war. It is reported to us in newspapers, magazines and on the air waves. Thank God for our free press. Without it, most of us would be unaware of the catastrophe upon us. The Japanese interviewed by *Business Week* (December 14, 1981) have revealed their plan for a take-over of Western markets in the 1980s. If you have not already done so, Mr President, we urge you and the members of Congress to read the *Business Week* article, 'Japan's Strategy For The '80s'.

The American Way

The American economy today does not have a chance in head-on competition with the Japanese. Why? Because the Japanese society — government, banking, labor, education — supports business, in every way. In the United States, business and labor have become the target of society — a target of our government through archaic and repressive legislation, of a monetary policy which imposes impossible rates of interest. Some of the very policies — designed to protect American industry and consumers from unfair practices — destroy us when we deal internationally. These laws enable other countries to take our technology with impunity. This situation, coupled with the Japanese Government's subsidies and business support, puts American industry on the road to bankruptcy.

Japan, AT&T, IBM and the Auto Industry

Never would the Japanese government have permitted the dismemberment of AT&T: the best communication system in the world; a company which took 100 years to build. A company, which, with its dedicated management and employees, and its technological contributions has contributed so much to the growth and greatness of America. Our government harassed IBM in court for thirteen years, causing incalculable damage, and has now found the case to be without merit. Japan would never try to cut the heart out of a successful business. If this anti-business trend continues, our auto industry will be gone to Japan within three to five years, with 20% of the American work force directly affected . . . their strategy also calls for the takeover of the computer and communications industries in the '80s.

Japanese Education vs. American Education

I understand, Mr President, that for every 1,000 engineers graduated from Japan's universities, there are 100 law school graduates. In the U.S.A., for every 1,000 engineers, there are 10,000 lawyers graduated. I also understand there are 40,000 lawyers in all of Japan. In the U.S.A., a recent tally indicates we have 480,000 lawyers. How do they exist? The answer — corporations, government regulations, audits, reports, taxes, legislation, litigation and bankruptcy. This adds great costs to our economy, eventually to products and services mounting to billions a year. Public accounting firms (Congress legislated them into prominence by enactment of the Securities and Exchange Act in 1933–34) provide the mandated audits of corporate financial reports. In 1980, fees of only eight major accounting firms added $6 billion to the corporate cost of doing business.

The public accounting firm that audits General Motors reportedly assigns a team of 1,400 accountants, spread through offices around the world, for the field work. This team alone, according to Mark Stevens in his book, *The Big Eight*, is larger than 99 percent of all of the accounting firms in the world. This cost is reflected in the cost of GM cars. Japan has no such legislation.

Every government regulation adds to every product cost. Interstate Commerce Commission rulings for one year alone, required 57,027 pages of fine print in the Federal Register. Currently, U.S. business spends over $120 billion annually to complete paper work required by the government. It is not that I am against lawyers and accountants. I believe that their talents can be redirected toward constructive work to help us to rebuild this nation.

On The Other Side of The Coin

Mr President, if anyone had told me a decade ago that my small company, TII, (with annual sales of $21 million) would have more pre-tax income than four of the largest automobile companies combined, I would have laughed them out of my office. Our good fortune is due in part to the government of Puerto Rico and to our high technology, 'quality award' winning, highly productive and creative labor force. The government there has developed an enlightened tax policy — a tax moratorium to companies locating there — to strengthen the Puerto Rican economy. As you so eloquently told us in 1980, 'These loyal Americans have proved themselves in every war since 1898', and, Mr President, they know how to fight this one.

You may know, Mr. President, the little town of Toa Alta in Puerto Rico. In 1974, 30 percent of the population of that town was out of work. The Commonwealth Government gave us every encouragement to locate a factory there. We began with 20 people and now, seven years later, over 450 people are working in that factory. They pay taxes, have savings accounts, buy homes and cars, and send their well-fed, happy children to school. This economic success story can be repeated throughout the United States of America.

Meeting the Challenge

Many of our fellow Americans express a growing feeling that nothing can be done to reverse this tide and that we will become a colonial dependency of Japan. I do not agree. Something *can* be done, Mr President. Let us put partisanship aside. We must move boldly and quickly to remove from business and agriculture the restrictions and regulations that are bankrupting them. Help us to get back to where we were with free enterprise — the enterprise that built this nation in 175 years from a backwoods frontier to the wealthiest and most charitable nation in the history of mankind. Trust the people. Bring us together. There are 226,504,825 Americans, rich in bright intellect from every race and culture in the world, who have one thing in common, the love of freedom. It is freedom which inspires creativity and productivity. Send out the call for the dollar-a-year men and women. We are still here — ready, willing and able. We have the know-how and the patriotism and I believe, we have some of the answers. We look forward to the day when government, labor, banking, industry, agriculture and education will again work together for the full employment of our people.

May I express admiration and gratitude, Mr President, for your leadership and the cooperation you have received from our Congressmen. We need their understanding and their help in this fight for survival and the right to be free. Talk to us Mr President. Give us the needed inspiration and leadership. Then, God willing, the people of this once most powerful nation will waken Uncle Sam to flex his economic muscles and rise again to greatness.

With many good wishes for you health and success, I am
Respectfully yours,

Alfred J. Roach
Chairman of the Board
TII Industries, Inc.

Open Letter as it appeared in the *International Herald Tribune* Wednesday, 28 May 1997

What will the Children Ask?
Reflections on the Marshall Plan and our Future

On March 9th of this year, I published an Open Letter to the leaders of the world in *The New York Times*; and ten days later, it appeared in the *International Herald Tribune*. My message emphasized that there are tens of thousands of nuclear weapons poised in silos throughout Russia and the adjacent republics of Belarus, Kazakhstan and Ukraine. I appealed to world leaders to act decisively and to prevent the chilling possibility that even one of these weapons would find their way into the hands of a despot. This anniversary of the Marshall Plan is an ideal opportunity to amplify my earlier message: to avert the catastrophe of nuclear crime, we must bring Russia and the surrounding republics into the fold of <u>stable</u> democratic nations. *Moreover, without substantial further aid and investment from the world's most developed economies, that stability will be nearly impossible to obtain.*

After reading my Open Letter in March, my granddaughter Stacey, came into my study with her eight-month-old son poised on her arm. He was napping peacefully, but Stacey looked pensive. She asked me,

'What kind of world, Grandfather, can my child expect to grow up in?'

What world, indeed? Such are the question of today . . . and those yet to come. I often think about the questions our great-grandchildren will ask in Web-site college classrooms decades from now. I'm frightened when I imagine what some of those questions might be, but I think it's far better to pose those questions today and reflect on them . . . and not compel our grandchildren to ask them when the tragic answers are part of unchangeable history:

- 'You mean world leaders couldn't see that the intelligentsia of Russia's enormous military and scientific establishment were cut loose from jobs and opportunities and that a critical few would sell skills and materials to the highest bidder?'

- 'You're telling us that no one foresaw that the East Bloc nuclear arsenal offered exactly the weapons that terrorist groups and rogue nations wanted desperately to command?'

- 'You're asking us to believe that a large piece of the world became a contaminated, radioactive cinder because we weren't smart enough to fund a transition to post-Cold War peace?'

Russia, Risk, and Reality

As we celebrate the fiftieth anniversary of the Marshall Plan, we would do well to look back and ask ourselves: Why and how did the Marshall Plan work? The Marshall Plan should be a model that occurs to us whenever dramatic changes and transitions occur. It is a model that may have even greater bearing on the 1990s than it did in the 1940s.

In his watershed work entitled *Diplomacy*, Henry Kissinger offers these insights about the Marshall Plan:

- Secretary Marshall began by dispassionately analyzing 'the relationship between the proposed aid program and the American interests' in a key Oval Office session with Congressional leaders.

- '. . . Secretary Marshall, in a commencement address at Harvard . . . committed America to the task of eradicating the social and economic conditions that tempted aggression. America would aid European recovery, announced Marshall, to avoid "political disturbances" and "desperation", to restore the world economy, and to nurture free institutions.'

- 'The Atlantic Alliance served as a military bulwark against Soviet expansion, while the Marshall Plan strengthened Western Europe economically and socially.'

Several themes that I draw from Dr Kissinger's comments deserve special emphasis: George Marshall could project a *dispassionate* understanding of how helping Europe bolstered *American interests,* and adverse *social and economic conditions* have real power to tempt aggression.

As experts have pointed out, American support for the integrated economic recovery of Western Europe, including Germany, created the foundation for a Common Market. Without that Market, the peace that World War II achieved could never have been sustained. The Marshall Plan's monumental role in changing world history was not a function of its goodwill or its humanity, but of clear and objective reasoning about what constitutes the threats on our horizon.

For several years, I have advocated replicating the Marshall Plan in our time for Russia and other successor republics to the Soviet Union. Western public opinion has concluded — and falsely, I might add — that the principal threat to Western and American interests has vanished. It has not. Rather, the threat has become stealthily shifting both the components and the finished weapons of colossal destructive power into the marketplace of terrorism and rogue nations.

Provoking Nuclear Catastrophe

If we don't actively address the social and economic conditions that tempt aggressions, we expose our vital interests to extreme risk. There may be as many as 40,000 Russian nuclear warheads yet to be deactivated. Graham T. Allison and his colleagues warn in the penetrating study *Avoiding Nuclear Anarchy*, 'The single most important truth about the post-Cold War security environment is that Russia is convulsed by a genuine, ongoing revolution . . . But about the current revolution, there is one difference without precedent in human experience. Never before has a superpower arsenal of nuclear weapons and fissile material existed in the midst of an ongoing (and unavoidably turbulent) revolution . . . *the risk of nuclear detonation on American soil has increased.*'

Brian Eads, in a memorable *Reader's Digest* (April, 1997) article titled 'A Shopping Mall for Nuclear Blackmailers', cites a multitude of frightening examples. I quote just two of them below:

- 'According to U.S. Senate testimony, retired Russian naval captain Alexei Tikhomirov slipped through an unguarded gate at a nuclear-fuel storage facility near Murmansk in 1993. He sawed a padlock off a door, then pried it open with a metal bar. Inside he broke off ten pounds of uranium from three submarine fuel-assemblies, stuffed the material into a bag and calmly retraced his steps. Eight months later police caught him by chance as he tried to sell the stolen uranium. (Asking price: $50,000.) The military prosecutor remarked that "potatoes were guarded better than naval fuel."'

• 'According to . . . Graham Allison, more nuclear material has been stolen from the former Soviet Union since the fall of the Berlin Wall than the United States produced in the first three years of the Manhattan Project — and that's counting only the known incidents.'

Project Sapphire* and other security control programs are important steps, just as the founding of NATO was a crucial adjunct to the Marshall Plan. But, control is not enough. As both Graham Allison and Brian Eads advocate, buying Russian HEU (heavily enriched uranium) at a faster pace and transforming it to civilian use is a wise step. But, in my view, they still fall short of a different need. And, that's where a Marshall Plan for Russia enters the picture.

Fifty years ago, the Marshall plan objectively created stability and curtailed the threat of aggression in post-War Europe. Isn't the stimulus of a Marshall Plan for economic development in Russia — a plan that truly harnesses and redirects the powerhouse of Russian technology — equally fundamental in our time?

George Marshall may have been a distinguished humanitarian. In my opinion, he made a greater contribution to humanity because he was something more; a dedicated pragmatist who recognized and addressed threats in a realistic way. Have we forgotten the real wisdom of this soldier-statesman from Uniontown, Pennsylvania? Do we dare to forget it now?

---

* U.S. Project Sapphire, successfully moved tons of fissionable materials, including enough weapon-grade material to build some two dozen nuclear bombs, from Kazakhstan to a plant in the U.S. for conversion into commercial fuel.

Index of Names